CLARK PUBLIC LIBRARY

3 9502 00145 8371

D0898163

813.54   Vickers, Graham.
Vic
         Chasing Lolita.

CLARK PUBLIC LIBRARY
303 WESTFIELD AVENUE
CLARK, NJ 07066
732-388-5999

CHASING LOLITA

HOW POPULAR CULTURE CORRUPTED NABOKOV'S LITTLE GIRL ALL OVER AGAIN

GRAHAM VICKERS

CHICAGO
REVIEW
PRESS

Clark Public Library - Clark, N. J.

813.54
Vic
10-28-08

Library of Congress Cataloging-in-Publication Data

Vickers, Graham.
  Chasing Lolita : how popular culture corrupted Nabokov's little girl all over again /
Graham Vickers.
    p. cm.
  The real life of Dolores Haze: just the facts—Casebooks and fantasies: Dolores Haze's
oft-told tale—A very 1950s scandal: hurricane Lolita—Lolita in movieland 1: little
victims and little princesses—Lolita in movieland 2: 'pedophilia is a hard sell'—On the
road: Lolita's moving prison—Take one: how did they ever make a film of Lolita?—Dramatic arts: Lolita center stage—The spirit of free enterprise: every foul poster—Tabloids
and factoids: the press and Lolita—Take two: once more with feeling—Blood sisters:
some responses to Lolita."
  Includes bibliographical references and index.
  ISBN 978-1-55652-682-4
  1. Nabokov, Vladimir Vladimirovich, 1899–1977 Lolita. 2. Nabokov, Vladimir
Vladimirovich, 1899–1977—Characters—Lolita. 3. Nabokov, Vladimir Vladimirovich,
1899–1977—Film and video adaptations. 4. Popular culture—United States—History—
20th century. 5. Popular culture—United States—History—21st century. 6. Literature
and society—United States—History—20th century. 7. Literature and society—United
States—History—21st century. 8. Lolita (Fictitious character). 9. Girls in literature. 10.
Nymphets in literature I. Title.

  PS3527.A15L6375 2008
  813'.54—dc22

2007052046

Interior design: Sarah Olson

© 2008 by Graham Vickers
All rights reserved
Published by Chicago Review Press, Incorporated
814 North Franklin Street
Chicago, Illinois 60610
ISBN: 978-1-55652-682-4
Printed in the United States of America

5 4 3 2 1

Clark Public Library - Clark, N. J.

To Jacqui

Thanks go to my editor Yuval Taylor for supporting this book from the start and helping to guide it to publication.

"My poor *Lolita* is having a rough time."

——Vladimir Nabokov, writing to Graham Greene

CONTENTS

INTRODUCTION

LOLITA WAS PROMISCUOUS! LOLITA WAS HOT! LOLITA WAS JAIL-bait! Right?

Wrong. Separating the miss from the myth is the ultimate aim of this book. I have approached the task first by giving the Lolita of Nabokov's novel a more objective appraisal than its solipsistic narrator, Humbert Humbert, was able to do. I have then explored some of Lolita's predecessors in real life, in books, and in movies, not only because their examples colored the way people would come to view Lolita, but also because they themselves would later come to be viewed in the retrospective light of Nabokov's famous novel. In fact, the 1958 American publication date of *Lolita* may be considered less of a starting point and more of a literary lighthouse located in the pivotal center of the twentieth century, casting its light backward as well as forward.

I have gone on to explore some of the many copied and counterfeited Lolitas for what they and their creators might tell us about the capricious nature of our changing popular culture. Here are tawdry gewgaws (dolls, cosmetics, clothes, sunglasses, toys, and scarcely believable novelty items) as well as numerous artistic and quasi-artistic attempts to reincarnate her in other media, for other audiences, and for other times.

The original spark of inspiration for this book was a little less ambitious. It came from a moment in a BBC television documentary that was originally broadcast to coincide with the release of the 1997 film version of *Lolita*. Adrian Lyne's movie (the second of two film adaptations) had, to the surprise of many, enjoyed the willing consultative participation of Dmitri Nabokov, the author's dauntingly accomplished son, a famously rigorous critic of any attempts to fool around with his father's masterpiece. At one point in the documentary, as I recall, Nabokov fils showed the camera some tacky plastic Lolita-branded doll and offered his opinion that there was surely a book to be written about the bizarre and kitschy nature of the Lolita legacy. He added that this was not, however, a book that he himself would be writing. Yet such a book seemed to me to be a worthwhile enterprise, if only—I thought at the time—to explore the ramifications of the breakdown of cultural class distinctions that *Partisan Review* editor Frederick W. Dupee credited *Lolita* with bringing about, uniting highbrows and lowbrows, and making "the fading smile of the Eisenhower Age . . . give way to a terrible grin." After all, one of the first Lolita dolls was dreamed up by none other than the playwright Edward Albee for use in his ill-starred play of Nabokov's novel. Even *Lolita*'s author, Vladimir Vladimirovich Nabokov himself—a ruined Russian aristocrat, a world-famous lepidopterist, a distinguished academic, and a sublime novelist who detested second-rate art—hugely enjoyed newspaper cartoons, comic strips, and movie comedies, and could bring a scholarly (not to say sometimes pedantic) precision to discussions with his wife Véra as to whether they had seen a certain item years before on the Jack Paar show or that of Mike Douglas. Nabokov corresponded with Alfred Hitchcock, socialized with Peter Ustinov and James Mason, and at a Hollywood party once even met John

Wayne—although The Duke's oeuvre did seem to lie outside the cultural orbit of Lolita's author, who innocently asked him what he did for a living ("I'm in movies," Wayne is said to have replied). After meeting her, Nabokov declared fifties starlet and Elvis co-star Tuesday Weld "a charming ingénue, but not my idea of Lolita," while his uproarious laughter in a Cambridge movie theater that was showing John Huston's eccentric thriller *Beat the Devil* was noted as exceptionally disruptive even by those regular members of the cinema's audience—many of them students—who were quite accustomed to their distinguished professor's uncontrolled laughter in the dark.

Half a century or so later, in Lolita's name the world has now been given erotic lithographs and weird fashion movements, artful spin-off novels and miscellaneous movies, awkward theater dramatizations and ill-judged musical entertainments, and vile Internet subcultures and lurid newspaper clichés. (We may, I think, give LoLIta—a name recently coined in the tradition of TriBeCa and SoHo, in this case to signify Manhattan's Lower Little Italy district—the benefit of the doubt; Lolita Haze, conceived in Mexico, always had more of a Hispanic aura about her.)

In trying to redress the imbalance of Lolita's popular reputation and explore her susceptibility to being misunderstood, it is always worth keeping a single image in mind—that of a certain Russian writer standing at a lectern or rickety table in rented lodgings (or in one famous instance using a suitcase balanced on a bidet as his writing desk when times were hard and furnishings scarce), carefully conjuring a host of imaginary circumstances and characters on index cards, in pencil, in longhand, all across Europe and America. Lolita and her story were just one of these dazzling inventions, completed and put away in late 1953 and at once, in its author's mind, displaced by the next pressing project. If proof were needed it is furnished by the following anecdote. At the height of *Lolita's* first phenomenal success in the bestsellers, Nabokov was a guest speaker at the Herald Tribune's Book and Author Luncheon at the Waldorf-Astoria hotel in New York City. There he read his poem "An Evening of Russian Poetry" and sat down again, making no mention of *Lolita* at all. His nymphet's global fame, and by association his own, was a distant and unlikely prospect. In Nabokov's case—and perhaps in everyone's case—this was entirely as it should be, since fame tends to destroy people who pursue it for its own sake. Fame is of assistance only to people who make their work, not celebrity status, the point of their endeavors. "It is Lolita, not I, who is famous," Nabokov once said, when pressed, but her fame brought him wealth and independence, and if the suspicion remains that he would have preferred to have been rewarded earlier and more evenly for a lifetime of remarkable literary achievement, he was philosophical about the irony.

The German poet Rainer Maria Rilke defined fame as "the sum total of all the misunderstandings that can gather around one name." Surely no better definition has yet been devised, and no more graphic example of the phenomenon exists than what happened to Dolores Haze in the half century after she died.

[1]

THE REAL LIFE OF DOLORES HAZE:
Just the Facts

"Humbert Humbert is a middle-aged, fastidious college profes-sor. He also likes little girls. And none more so than Lolita, who [*sic*] he'll do anything to possess. Is he in love or insane, a silver-tongued poet or a pervert, a tortured soul or a monster—or is he all of these!"

THE ABOVE SUMMARY—EITHER SUPPLIED BY THE PUBLISHER OR staffers at the amazon.co.uk Web site on which it appears, promot-ing a Penguin Modern Classics edition of the novel—illustrates the difficulty of synopsizing the plot of *Lolita*. The book does not lend itself to literal précis. Most attempts to summarize it make it sound melodramatic or even absurd.

Structurally it is easy enough to outline. Nabokov's novel takes the form of a memoir supposedly written in prison by the self-styled Humbert Humbert, a European academic whose lifelong

sexual obsession with little girls has at last been fully indulged
with Lolita Haze, an American child who became his stepdaughter
after a series of unlikely schemes, accidents, and coincidences. The
colorful memoir is prefaced with a straitlaced introduction by the
fictitious John Ray Jr., who claims to be its appointed editor. The
novel's action takes place in various U.S. locations in the late 1940s
and early 1950s and presents Humbert and Lolita's story exclusively
from Humbert's point of view and in his own often florid literary
language.

So far, so good. It is when we come to summarize the book's
nature and texture that this infinitely subtle, allusive, comic, and
grotesque love story defeats us. "A black comedy about a middle-
aged man's obsession with a young girl" is the line most frequently
taken by movie listings journalists whom space compels to encap-
sulate the plot of either of the two film versions of *Lolita* in around
a dozen words. Such doomed exercises recall a sketch from the cult
1970s comedy TV series *Monty Python's Flying Circus* where, in the
setting of a televised competition, contestants are challenged to
give a fifteen-second summary of Proust's one-and-a-half-million-
word *À la recherche du temps perdu*. In the case of *Lolita*, though,
it is not the book's size but its elusive nature that defeats meaning-
ful summary; Lolita's life story has a narrator with an agenda and
his account is correspondingly light on facts, heavy on textures,
echoes, fantasies, fateful coincidences, and self-serving, passionate lies. Such irreducible material has always been anathema to the
popular media, where a snappy slogan is what's needed; today, in
the age of the sound bite, the elliptical impressionism of Humbert's
account leaves the heroine of *Lolita* even more susceptible to grotesque misinterpretations. Nabokov commentator Alfred Appel
Jr. offered a definitive example of how Lolita's racy reputation preceded her as long ago as 1955, when a fellow conscript at a U.S.
Army camp in France demanded to read Appel's copy of Nabokov's

"dirty book" (at that time solely published by the admittedly dubious Parisian imprint Olympia Press) only to fling it aside in disdain when the first paragraph confirmed his worst fears. "It's God-damn Litachure!!" was his contemptuous off-the-cuff review. Look at this tangle of thorns.

– – –

"You must be confusing me with some other fast little article," says Lolita to stepfather Humbert at one point late in their bleak relationship. Delivered as a riposte to his flawed recollection of one of her early crushes, her wry retort also stands as an unconscious prophecy and rebuke. After her death, Lolita was to become the patron saint of fast little articles the world over, not because Nabokov's mid-1950s novel depicted her as such but because, slowly and surely, the media, following Humbert's unreliable lead, cast her in that role.

The 1950s, a decade superficially so orderly and conformist, was already fomenting social change just below the surface. Overt social revolution might still be some way off, but in what was already beginning to look like a complex postwar world, the popular press and TV were starting to favor simple symbols. The public, they reasoned, wanted cartoonish representatives of complicated things. Accordingly, in the popular imagination wild-haired Albert Einstein became the Wacky European Scientist, surly Marlon Brando the Mumbling Ambassador of Inarticulate Youth, pneumatic Marilyn Monroe the paradigmatic Hollywood Pinup, mad-eyed bald man Pablo Picasso the Famous Modern Artist, and so on. It was a kind of visual shorthand, and it was often accompanied by editorial to match. If this trend did not actually discourage serious debate about science, acting, stardom, and modern art, neither did it do much to promote it. In this breezy spirit Lolita would gradually exemplify the Sultry Teenage Temptress. It was a travesty from the start.

In the first place, Lolita was a twelve-year-old child—not a teenager—when she first succumbed to the middle-aged man who subsequently narrated the saga of his infatuation with her. In the second place, she was not equipped, in any sense, to be an iconic temptress. The novel's descriptions of her stress her physical appeal but only in relation to Humbert's appetites. That appeal owes nothing to any broadly recognizable popular image of a siren, past or present, but exclusively to the lineaments of unformed adolescence—delicate shoulder blades, long tapering toes, and the musky scents not of seductive perfumes but of unwashed hair. In short, far from being overt, Lolita's sex appeal would have been elusive to all but a pedophile with a very specific shopping list of expectations. For Humbert, the first wave of desire for Lolita derived from her resemblance to a particular girl who obsessed him when he was fourteen and whose loss, he fancies, froze his sexual ideal forever, just as a snapshot freezes its subject in time as well as space.

In fact, there is no indication in Nabokov's novel that Lolita looked in any way overtly seductive, that she dressed to provoke, or that her sexual appetites were significantly different from those of her 1940s classmates. It was not until a publicity poster appeared for Stanley Kubrick's 1962 film of *Lolita* that we first encounter a color photograph of an entirely bogus Lolita wearing red heart-shaped sunglasses while licking a red lollipop (love and fellatio, get it?). Lolita's sunglasses in Kubrick's (black-and-white) film sport regular frames and at no point does she suck that kind of lollipop, so the poster makes false promises on every level. The same synthetic image subsequently graced many international paperback editions of the novel. Yet before *Lolita's* first American publication in 1958, Nabokov had insisted that there should be no little girl at all on the book's cover because he was in the business of writing about subjective rapture, not objective sexualization.

Bert Stern's famous photo of Sue Lyon defined the posters for Kubrick's 1962 film all over the world. It marks the first blatant visual travesty of Nabokov's grubby chestnut-haired twelve-year-old and does not even resemble the way Sue Lyon looks in the movie.

The Olympia Press edition of *Lolita* (the one that the good soldier Appel bought on the Left Bank of Paris) had automatically appeared as one in a uniform series of generally risqué novels sharing neutral typographical livery, but Nabokov's concerns were about the first American hardcover edition of 1958—the edition that was to launch its notoriety on a wider public—and were fully heeded: the front cover design was typographic, with no representational image at all. Before we venture, however, beyond the hearts-and-lollipops checkpoint and on into an infinite hall of Lolita-distorting mirrors, it seems worth pausing to consider a slogan made famous by a program that was just beginning its run of phenomenal popularity even as the short, sad life of Dolores Haze was coming to an end.

Nabokov insisted there should
be no picture of a little girl
on the first U.S. hardcover
edition of *Lolita* in I958. The
cover reference to *Pnin* (published in I957) was a preemptive bid to position *Lolita* as
another novel from a respected
writer, not some one-off bid
for a scandalous success. (G.P.
Putnam's Sons first edition of
Lolita)

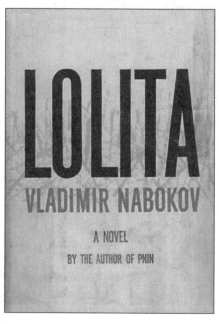

Almost all later editions of
Lolita ignored Nabokov's wishes
about the cover and included an
image of a girl. This recent one
from Penguin UK continues the
tradition and features a model
and pose intended to evoke
Dominique Swain's Lolita from
the I997 film version. (Penguin
Modern Classics edition)

Inspired by the 1948 movie *He Walked by Night*, a film noir with a climactic gun battle in the storm drains of Los Angeles (recalling his moviegoing days with Lolita and her mother, Humbert describes with scathing enjoyment the atmosphere of profligate but inaccurate gunplay in gangster films where villains were chased through sewers), the cop show *Dragnet* became a big U.S. hit on both radio and TV. A clever Stan Freberg parody ("St. George and the Dragonet") topped the record charts in 1953 and made the show even more famous than it already was. Presented in a spare documentary style and featuring the trademark monotone delivery of its lead actor and creator Jack Webb, the show was a police procedural with a catchphrase. Faced with yet another witness's fanciful recollection of the crime under investigation, Webb, playing Sergeant Joe Friday of the L.A.P.D., would routinely interrupt with, "All we want are the facts, ma'am. Just the facts."

— — —

A few facts, then. On her twelfth birthday Dolores Haze was fifty-seven inches tall, weighed seventy-eight pounds, and had an IQ of 121. Her "vital statistics" (to use an idiom of the time) were 27-23-29, that is to say, twenty-seven inches (chest), twenty-three inches (waist), and twenty-nine inches (hips). Surprisingly, there is more. Her thigh girth was seventeen inches, her calf girth eleven inches (as was the circumference of her neck), and she was still in possession of her vermiform appendix.

This clinical standard of objectivity is not typical of the information to be found elsewhere in the novel. Instead, *Lolita* is shot through with the skewed perspective and dazzling prose style of its narrator, the self-styled Humbert Humbert, a Swiss-English professor and pedophile recently relocated to the United States from Europe. Capricious Humbert, however, does share Nabokov's miraculous eye for detail, and so, here and there, Lolita's "real life" does stubbornly shine through the miasma of his self-serving narrative, and we can certainly extract a certain amount of factual (or at least fairly objective) data that seem not to have been unduly colored by the narrator's highly partial perspective.

We can be fairly sure, for example, that Dolores Haze was born on January 1, 1935, in Pisky, a disguised midwestern town located in an area noted for producing hogs, corn, and coal. We even know that she was conceived in Veracruz, Mexico, the occasion being the 1934 spring honeymoon of midwesterners Harold E. Haze and his bride Charlotte, née Becker. Harold and Charlotte's second successful attempt to reproduce took place in 1937 (location unrecorded) and in due course resulted in a blond-haired boy who would die at the age of two. This was to be the first of two family losses for Charlotte, who nevertheless treated Dolores, her surviving offspring, as a constantly nagging nuisance. Long before the routine conflicts between mother and preteen child might have been expected to surface, Charlotte was at loggerheads with her daughter. In a diary entitled *A Guide to Your Child's Development* she would neutrally record Dolores's height, weight, and intelligence quotient as above but then go on to identify her twelve-year-old child's personality as "aggressive . . . distrustful . . . irritable . . . obstinate"—and all the other negative options on offer in the evenhanded menu supplied by the authors of the guide. It seemed the death of her husband had cast a pall over Charlotte's life that would not lift until she met her second spouse, at which point daughter Dolores would simply become a renewed source of intrusion and annoyance. Already a voice other than that of narrator Humbert appears to be weighting the evidence against Lolita.

We learn very few facts about Harold E. Haze's life or premature death from our narrator. After his death Charlotte apparently moved east almost immediately to live in what had been her mother-in-law's house in the town of Ramsdale in an unnamed New England state we may assume to be New Hampshire. Now a widow in her midthirties, frustrated Charlotte set up home in a modest white frame house at 342 Lawn Street to begin a new life with her aggressive, distrustful, irritable, obstinate daughter. Then, in what she almost certainly saw as a divinely motivated second chance at happiness (Charlotte was, we shall discover, a humorlessly spiritual woman), fate delivered a cultured European academic, handsome twin-named Humbert Humbert right to her door. A nearby house in which Humbert was to have lodged had been portentously destroyed by fire the night before his arrival in Ramsdale, and so he had been hastily rerouted to the Haze home by his intended landlord, who believed that Charlotte too was looking for a tenant.

Humbert, the son of a Swiss father and English mother, was an academic who had inherited a small business in New York that now more or less ran itself. His only reason for moving out of the city and going to Ramsdale in the first place had been to rent a quiet place in New England where he could work undisturbed on a book of French grammar. As deeply unimpressed by 342 Lawn Street as he was by its owner, Humbert had already resolved to decline the unsought offer of lodging there when he was overwhelmed by his first glimpse of Lolita. This four-foot nine, seventy-eight pound, twelve-year-old child of the Midwest was sunning herself in the Lawn Street yard, as happily oblivious to this dark stranger's sudden U-turn about lodging there as she was to his lifelong obsession with a certain type of little girl aged between nine and fourteen and in possession of a certain fey sexual charisma, a type he dubbed "nymphets."

— — —

So Dolores—variously nicknamed Lo, Lola, Dolly, and Lolita depending on the social context—was the ultimate embodiment of all the nymphets Humbert had ever desired and his sole reason for moving into 342 Lawn Street. Yet, as Charlotte's lodger, Humbert soon grudgingly allowed himself to be cast in the role his landlady had intended for him all along: that of lover and then husband. With Lolita summarily dispatched to summer camp by her spiteful mother, Humbert and Charlotte married after knowing each other for less than two months. It was a fast and farcical affair driven by doomed impulses: Charlotte desperately wanted a classy husband and Humbert desperately wanted to be near Lolita, whom he assumed would be returning to the Ramsdale home at the end of the summer, so affording him surreptitious opportunities to indulge his obsession. Almost at once his cynical plan began to unravel, and as it happened to some extent had already been preempted by someone whose presence was so far completely unknown to him. For Humbert was not alone in his desire; another middle-aged man with more than a passing interest in nymphets had his eye on her too.

Clare Quilty, born in New Jersey and educated at Columbia University, was a successful playwright, darkly good-looking in the same way that Humbert was, and, to boot, a minor media celebrity. Quilty even promoted a brand of cigarettes in magazine advertisements. He had a dentist uncle who lived in Ramsdale and, through this connection, had been a guest speaker at Charlotte's women's club before Humbert ever arrived on the scene. What is more, Quilty had already lasciviously fondled ten-year-old Lolita on his lap over two years before Humbert managed, eventually, to improve on the trick on the Haze sofa, ejaculating, he assures us, without Lolita ever being aware of his elaborately disguised indulgence. Quilty, however, was to remain an almost completely unknown quantity to Humbert for another five years.

When Charlotte dropped the bombshell that she had decided to send her daughter away to boarding school as soon as summer camp ended, she abruptly abolished Humbert's sole reason for entering into the marriage in the first place. Threatened with permanent separation from the child he desired, Humbert found himself marooned with the wife he never wanted in a smug little town he hated. Desperate to rid himself of Charlotte, he wildly contemplated murder, lost his nerve, and then disbelievingly found himself the beneficiary of a near-miraculous stroke of fate when Charlotte was killed in a freak automobile accident.

Dolores, still at camp in a neighboring state, was now officially an orphan, although Humbert delayed telling her the fatal news when he went to collect her from camp, telling her instead that her mother was hospitalized with a serious but not fatal illness. He took his newly acquired stepdaughter to a hotel some four hours' drive from her camp, where he planned to drug and have sex with her before they drove back to Ramsdale the following morning. The drug failed to work, but to Humbert's delighted astonishment they had sex anyway. Lolita complied—and in the end even initiated the proceedings—in a spirit of casual mischief that probably owed something to the lingering resentment she felt toward the mother she had no reason to believe would not recover. Humbert's stepdaughter had anyway, it turned out, been experimenting with sex at camp and had not failed to notice Humbert's desperate longing. In their hotel room, she shared with him matter-of-fact confidences about those tentative erotic games at camp (sex, Lolita concluded evenly, was good for the complexion) and made it clear that her youthful explorations were neither uncommon nor unduly precocious. The next morning Humbert told her that her mother was dead.

Up to this point Lolita's list of known sexual encounters is as follows: she has been fondled by a couple of middle-aged men who like little girls; she has been tutored in kissing by Elizabeth Talbot, a school friend; she has had some mechanical sex with Charlie Holmes, the thirteen-year-old son of the camp mistress (her cautious appraisal of Charlie's attentions is that it was "sort of fun"); and she has now had sex with her stepfather, who, having strained every nerve to contrive the intimacy, concludes that she was the one who seduced him. In the brief future that lies before her (she will be dead at seventeen), Lolita will effectively be incarcerated for a year in the series of motels and automobiles that Humbert deploys to avoid staying in any one place where their strange relationship might be detected for what it is. She will fall in love with her old hero, Clare Quilty, who will quickly dump her for not participating in his drug-fueled orgies. And she will marry and carry the child of a nice guy with no money and a severe hearing disability. Some fast little article.

– – –

The facts. In his foreword to *Lolita*, Humbert's editor, Dr. John Ray Jr., says that the curious may look up the facts of his client's crime in the relevant local newspapers for 1952. Exactly what actualities might be revealed by such researches? We might expect to find, under a New Hampshire, late September dateline, the news that a forty-two-year-old French professor faced a murder charge after the bullet-riddled body of Clare Quilty, a well-known playwright, had been discovered at his family home twelve miles north of the town of Parkington. Otherwise any account of Professor Humbert's subsequent arraignment in connection with the fatal shooting of the forty-one-year-old New Jersey–born writer would be rather short on background detail. There might perhaps be mention of a short police chase that ended when the suspect's automobile ran off the road and into a field. An unnamed guest present at the Quilty home might be quoted as saying that a stranger fitting Humbert's description had admitted that he had just killed Quilty before calmly leaving the house and driving away. There would be absolutely no mention, however, of Lolita Haze. When all is said and done, she was Humbert's private tragedy as much as he was hers.

Later, in his prison cell, awaiting trial, Humbert would inform his future readers that if he were his own judge, he would give himself at least thirty years for rape and dismiss the rest of the charges, including that of Quilty's murder.

Significantly, Lolita would also be missing from the factual testimonies of many other people who might be called upon to serve on any terrestrial or celestial jury. From the moment her mother died unexpectedly, Lolita effectively fell off society's radar, existing for a year as nothing more than Daddy's pet traveling companion, an itinerant preteen consumer with an insatiable appetite for novelty motel cabins, radio music, hot fudge sundaes, Wurlitzer jukeboxes, clothes, shoes, magazines, movies, souvenirs, candies, comics, and Places of Interest That Had to Be Visited during their twenty-seven-thousand-mile, serpentine road trip whose destination was the same as its starting point. Hundreds of motel proprietors, waitresses, salespersons, and other commercially motivated suppliers of goods and services must all have smiled at her, the fifth, tenth, or twentieth little girl of the day, but they had no reason to wonder about what happened in the motel cabins at night. At no point did the law or the education authorities ever suspect that she was trapped in an enforced sexual relationship with her stepfather, nor did her public behavior otherwise suggest that she was anything other than a sturdy, healthy, decidedly homely kid (as her late mother once described her) with conventional preteen appetites, a child who was touring the United States with her attentive dad during a gap between grade school and high school.

The real-life case of an eleven-year-old New Jersey kid who shared Lolita's fate (of which more later) strongly reinforces that scenario. When Lolita finally walked out of Humbert's life during a short reprise of that trip some months later, it was not into the

care of the state that she went but into the arms of another pedophile—playwright, pornographer, and drug addict Clare Quilty—
who soon ditched her, leaving her to drift for a couple of years doing
menial work in a string of small towns before finally opting for the
harbor of a safe marriage.

The facts, it seems, only get us so far after all. They let us picture
a chestnut-haired child of the 1940s, a conventional mix of charm
and vulgarity and predictable appetites, but in no way a temptress
in *status pupa*. They can show us a tangle of chance and circumstance in the midst of which an ingenious pervert tries to rearrange
the world to suit his obsession. But to appreciate something of Lolita's greater claim to our sympathy—greater than our suspicion that
she was to some extent the author of her own misfortune—we have
no choice but to turn to Humbert as our main authority. Despite
his crimes and his outrageous solipsism, he remains something of
a poet with a poet's eye for detail. If his obsession usually acts as a
distorting lens through which he depicts Lolita, he is still capable,
here and there, of documenting his nymphet's day-to-day life more
or less objectively, and his occasional insights and sympathy for her
plight can come as a shocking surprise—shocking because even
when he is sensitive enough to pity her, self-interest usually undercuts his compassion. He admits, for example, to moments of acute
postcoital compassion toward Lolita, gathering her in his arms with
selfless tenderness only to immediately reawaken his own lust. Lolita would groan in disbelief, and the wave of compassion would be
replaced by another sort.

Two particular incidents recounted by Humbert give acute
insight into the unexpressed pain of Lolita's captive childhood and
her captor's very conditional sensitivity toward it. Both incidents
take place in late 1948 in the hiatus between two road trips when
Humbert has been obliged to set up a travesty of a family home in
the New England college town of Beardsley where Lolita is sup-

posed to continue her education at the local high school. Ever fearful of exposure, Humbert tries to control all aspects of Lolita's life, and in this atmosphere even the most innocent of social encounters poses a potential threat of exposure.

At one point suspicious Humbert feels reluctantly obliged to invite into their parlor one of Lolita's new friends, plump young Avis Byrd, who has come calling with her father. Humbert sees Lolita switch on the dazzling social smile she reserves for strangers as she leans on a table and plays idly with a heavy fruit knife lying there. Neighborly pleasantries are exchanged. Then Humbert notes how a spontaneous show of affection by Avis toward her dad—who reciprocates—causes the light to go out of Lolita's smile just as the fruit knife falls and strikes her painfully on the ankle. Her cry, Humbert knows, is triggered by the physical pain, but her subsequent tears are tears of raw envy for plump, lumpy Avis, "who had such a wonderful fat pink dad and a small chubby brother, and a brand-new baby sister, and a home, and two grinning dogs, and Lolita had nothing."

The second incident also takes place in their temporary Beardsley home and concerns an evening when Lolita, who has been reading by the fire, puts down her book and, with forced casualness, tries to get Humbert to talk about her dead mother. When he stonewalls her inquiries she dully abandons the attempt and goes to bed. Humbert picks up the book she was reading and discovers it to be the story of a girl whose dying mother heroically suppresses all show of affection for her daughter so that the child will not miss her when she is gone. Humbert coolly considers going after her to sympathize but thinks better of it; on balance he always prefers to keep a dispassionate distance from an emotional display.

Moments like these give glimpses of Lolita's unexpressed pain, and just because Humbert rations them in his memoir does not mean that they might not have been more numerous. For the main part, his most objective appreciations of his stepdaughter are to do with how conventional he finds her appetites, how unsophisticated her enthusiasms, how vulgar her slang—in short how alien he finds her entire preteen world. Lolita, he tells us, particularly liked a popular song of the day—"Oh My Carmen, My Little Carmen" is his best guess at the title—and her enthusiasm for its trite rhymes and rhythms perplexes and amuses him even though he (who can quote lengthy passages of poetry and memorize verbatim his own long-lost diary entries) can somehow never quite remember the banal lyrics. He notes her almost religious devotion to the rites of youth: shopping for clothes, feeding totemic jukeboxes with handfuls of silver, devouring homiletic magazines for fashion and etiquette tips, and gorging herself on rich soda fountain foods that magically fail to blemish her complexion. He notes her unfeeling dismissiveness of a classmate, Ginny, the polio-stricken daughter of his intended landlord back in Ramsdale ("She's a fright. And mean. And lame.") and records that she has a morbid interest in press photographs of auto collisions. In this way we get a wealth of tiny incidental facts about Lolita from him: her rather unfastidious personal habits, the old scar on her calf caused by someone's roller skate, her taste for cherry red toenail polish, her increasing skill at domestic deceit after a spell of acting in a school play, and—a nice detail this—that she becomes Humbert's dedicated accomplice whenever they encounter a policeman.

Fact-loving policemen appear all through *Lolita*. Improbably timely patrolmen reach the scene of Charlotte's death on Lawn Street just yards from the house even before Humbert gets there because they were issuing parking tickets just two blocks away. The services of the local police are vouchsafed to find Lolita on a hiking trip when she is at camp, so jeopardizing Humbert's Machiavellian plan to collect and have sex with her before she finds out about her mother's death. Then a veritable swarm of policemen appears, albeit serially, during the illicit yearlong road trip. All pose a potential twin threat—imprisonment for Humbert and supposed institutional guardianship for Lolita—and whatever the prevailing mood between stepfather and stepdaughter, Lolita usually chips in to charm the admonitory traffic cop, or at least advise Humbert shrilly that running red lights and breaking the speed limit are not advisable responses to the sudden appearance of a patrol car. Nervy encounters with cops abound while Lolita remains in Humbert's captivity. Then, finally, when Humbert drives away from the scene of his murderous crime and nothing matters anymore, he does so at a sedate twenty miles an hour although, quite deliberately, on the wrong side of the road. His arrest is both inevitable and rather civilized.

Humbert does not tell of his subsequent interrogation, merely of his transition from psychopathic ward to prison cell, which is where he writes his memoir, the novel itself. He does, however, tell us that the full explanation everyone would like to hear will not be forthcoming during his trial since his memoir must remain under lock and key until Lolita Haze is no longer alive. Sergeant Joe Friday's East Coast colleagues, whom we may assume share his diligent insistence on "just the facts," would therefore be in possession of all the relevant facts—gun, murder, confession—but would have missed the essential point. Lolita was the point. Humbert's defiant, moody, bright, teasing, resentful, deceitful, vulgar, affectionate, duplicitous, likeable, fast little article was surely the innocent victim of his obsession—and her innocence can hardly be doubted simply because she did not always behave well. At least she retained her anonymity while she was alive, although it seems a poor reward given her short life span. What happened to her reputation afterward is, of course, another matter, and also the matter in hand.

Dragnet's other famous catchphrase, by the way, came in the form of a solemn rubric at the start of each episode, and it echoed a similar, if more wordy, pledge from John Ray Jr. at the start of *Lolita*.

"Only the names have been changed, to protect the innocent," Jack Webb would intone before the week's fiction got under way, implying documentary authenticity by means of solemn if unnecessary reassurance. Tensions between fact and fiction, real names and aliases, evocation and invention, description and advocacy, confession and fantasy not only run through *Lolita* from start to finish but also precede and postdate the novel in a sometimes extraordinary series of foreshadowings, overlaps, and echoes.

[2]

CASEBOOKS AND FANTASIES:
Dolores Haze's Oft-Told Tale

DID SHE HAVE A PRECURSOR? INDEED SHE DID; MANY OF THEM. IN the course of the novel Humbert himself helpfully offers several historical examples of what he says are notable sexual relationships between older men and very young girls. These are presented to support his breezy assertion that what outrages today's society may have been perfectly acceptable in earlier times or in other cultures. He has the grace to acknowledge that this does not lessen his crime in the eyes of contemporary U.S. law since he, like everyone else, must be judged by the standards of the day. Still, by casting himself alongside poets like Dante and Petrarch—not to mention Edgar Allan Poe—he seeks somehow to glamorize his wretched appetites by implying that his perversion is one to which artists and visionaries are particularly susceptible.

When Humbert makes a passing reference to Dante's "love" for the child Beatrice, he is being entirely misleading, implying that Dante Alighieri was an adult when he met the eight-year-old

Beatrice Portinari in 1274. Since Dante was only nine at the time (and there is no historical record of an affair between the couple at any point anyway), this is a dishonest ploy, to say the least. His Francesco Petrarch reference is even less persuasive, asserting that Petrarch fell madly in love with Laureen when she was a fair-haired child of twelve. The poet was twenty-three when he first became enamored of the mysterious Laura in Avignon's Église de Sainte Claire during the spring of 1327. Although evocatively immortalized in Petrarch's verse, historically speaking Laura remains an entirely unknown quantity. It is only some scholars' guess that she was in reality one Laura de Noves, the wife of Hugues de Sade. And even if this were true, then she was not only already married but also a mere six years younger than Petrarch, making her seventeen at the time of their meeting in that French church. All this shabby pseudohistorical sleight of hand suggests that Humbert's elaborate bid to align himself with two poets who ushered in the Renaissance is little more than an attempt to extenuate himself in the reader's eyes by means of benign cultural association. Humbert is, however, quite right when he says that Virginia Clemm was only thirteen when she married her twenty-seven-year-old cousin, the poet and mystery writer Edgar Allan Poe, in 1836.

Poe is something of an éminence grise always present in the shadows of Lolita. Humbert appropriates his first name as a decorative addition to his own when the fancy suits him ("Edgar H. Humbert" is how he signs in at the Enchanted Hunters Hotel). And in all there are over twenty references to Poe throughout the novel, some in the form of oblique allusions to the writer's novels and characters but most of them in connection with Annabel Lee, the heroine of Poe's most famous poem and near-namesake of Humbert's first love.

Humbert's grand theory is that his youthful obsession with one Annabel Leigh, a girl of his own age, lay at the root of his adult perversion. When the young couple had to part, their love was uncon-summated (both were age fourteen), and Humbert would have us believe that the event consigned him forever to try to re-create her in other young girls. Over the years the age gap between the fanta-sist and the time-arrested object of his fantasy inevitably widened so that by the time Humbert first encountered Lolita Haze sunbath-ing on the grass at 342 Lawn Street in 1947, he was thirty-seven, while this, his latest candidate for reincarnating Annabel, was two years younger than the original.

Poe's 1849 poem "Annabel Lee" supplies the plot and the seaside imagery, as well as the girl's name for young Humbert's ill-fated affair with his half-English, half-Dutch Annabel in the fateful sum-mer of 1923. "I was a child and she was a child," is Poe's line, seized upon by Humbert to stress the fact that he and Annabel Leigh were both young adolescents—coevals and equals—when they met by chance on the French Riviera where Humbert's father owned a hotel and Annabel's parents were vacationing. Young Humbert and Annabel became obsessively consumed by one another in the heat of their brief summer infatuation but were repeatedly thwarted in their attempts to have sex. In Poe's poem Annabel finally succumbs to a fatal chill right there in their "kingdom by the sea." Death also overtakes Humbert's Annabel, but not until after they have parted, and not in the Riviera sun—not until four months later when she dies of typhus in Corfu.

Poe's narrator philosophically sees Annabel Lee's spirit and his own as being comfortingly indivisible, even after her death.

> Neither the angels in Heaven above,
> Nor the demons down under the sea,
> Can ever dissever my soul from the soul
> Of the beautiful Annabel Lee.

Nabokov's narrator, by contrast, is inconsolable by spiritual musings and must try instead to reanimate his lost love in an unsatisfactory sequence of proxies—girl-children and young prostitutes—who will provide bleak solace across time and space, from adolescence to middle age and on two continents, until she is finally reincarnated in (and, ultimately, eclipsed by) Lolita Haze.

Leaving Humbert's own very selective literary and historical apologists to one side, we may, to use a Humbertian turn of phrase, "tom-peep" into the lives of a few more proto-Lolitas. The sexual appetites of Charles Lutwidge Dodgson, who under the name of Lewis Carroll found lasting fame as the author of *Alice's Adventures in Wonderland*, remain mired in ambiguity (the book was translated into Russian, incidentally, by a young Vladimir Nabokov, a daunting task for which he allegedly received the equivalent of five dollars). Despite what sound suspiciously like revisionist bids by friends and family to suppress information and generally sanitize Dodgson's memory, the British author's great fondness for children in general, and little girls in particular, is hard to regard as entirely innocent. In *Lewis Carroll: A Biography* (1995) Morton N. Cohen writes:

> We cannot know to what extent sexual urges lay behind Charles's preference for drawing and photographing children in the nude. He contended the preference was entirely aesthetic. But given his emotional attachment to children as well as his aesthetic appreciation of their forms, his assertion that his interest was strictly artistic is naïve. He probably felt more than he dared acknowledge, even to himself.

This sounds like a fair-to-generous analysis, given the evidence. It has repeatedly been suggested (without conclusive proof) that in 1863 Dodgson actually sought to marry eleven-year-old Alice Liddell and that this (failed) bid caused a serious family rift.

In an interview with *Wisconsin Studies*, Nabokov, an admirer of Carroll, said of him,

> Some odd scruple prevented me from alluding in *Lolita* to his wretched perversion and to those ambiguous photographs he took in dim rooms. He got away with it, as so many Victorians got away with pederasty and nympholepsy. His were sad, scrawny little nymphets, bedraggled and half-undressed, or rather semi-undraped, as if participating in some dusty and dreadful charade.

Alice Liddell photographed by Lewis Carroll. One of the author's most sentimental and unsettling photographs of his middle-class young muse has her dressed up as a ragged beggar girl with a come-hither look.

Whatever the truth of the matter, Alice Liddell was model both for Dodgson's famous literary heroine and for some rather more doubtful artistic projects: his studied photographs of children in general and Alice in particular—dressed and undressed— striking contrived poses in a series of theatrical tableaux. One of these photographs, entitled "Alice Liddell as the Beggar Child," now looks particularly dubious, being a picture in which young Alice's upper garments have been pulled down off her shoulders while she stands with a stony face, one hand on hip, the other cupped for alms. However contrived the setup, the effect is disturbingly suggestive: the child's assumed attitude and expression seem to convey rather too well that she knows what she may have to do for her coin. (Fellatio seeker, shameless briber, and moral escapologist Humbert notes, with a mix of admiration and censure, that during the span of a single school year Lolita manages to raise the bonus price of giving oral sex to four dollars.)

Dodgson died a bachelor in 1898, his reputation intact, perhaps because his fondness for young children was more commonplace than we might like to think and existed in an ambiguous Victorian moral climate where even honest attempts to protect children were based upon a very formal concept of sexual purity. In his book *Child-Loving: The Erotic Child and Victorian Culture*, James R. Kincaid went so far as to link our contemporary cultural preoccupations with pedophilia back to nineteenth-century "child protection" reforms that took the form of compulsory schooling, age of consent laws, and the formation of anticruelty societies. These initiatives, Kincaid argued, were all founded upon a well-meaning Victorian concept of childhood that was predicated on the notion of preserving children's sexual innocence. In doing so, such initiatives had the unintended consequence of establishing a definition of childhood that was largely sexual in its frame of reference, a definition that, he reasoned, was to bequeath future generations a sexually focused image of childhood. It is a nice point if something of an abstract one. Meanwhile, for the less fortunate children of the late nineteenth century, the growth of photography served mainly to fix forever the expressions of silent reproach on the faces of street urchins who had no need to rehearse their attitudes of deprivation and poverty for the documentary lens, as Alice Liddell and her friends occasionally did for Dodgson's delectation in his draped and shaded studio—a twilight chamber in every sense.

Early in the twentieth century came one of Lolita's almost forgotten progenitors. She was not famous at first and only attracted widespread attention in recent years—and then only because of the existence of her more famous successor. Heinz von Eschwege, a German author who wrote under the pen name of Heinz von Lichberg, invented his Lolita in 1916 in a short story of that name, which, in Carolyn Kunin's English translation, runs to a little under thirty-five hundred words. The coincidences beyond the title name are surprising, even though von Lichberg's tale is very unlike Nabokov's and his short but convoluted narrative resembles a set of those hollow Russian dolls that keep revealing ever smaller replicas of themselves stashed within. It begins with an account of a social gathering in Germany at which a professor tells the assembled company a story drawn from his own experience (or perhaps his reveries, he freely admits). This story is characterized by dreams and supernatural trans-generational coincidences. The German professor, traveling in Spain, is introduced to an Alicante innkeeper's daughter called Lolita, who "by our northern standards . . . was terribly young. . . . Her body was boyishly slim and supple and her voice was full and dark. But there was something more than her beauty that attracted me—there was a strange mystery about her that troubled me often on those moonlit nights." The couple have a sexual encounter and a brief affair and then part, but the story is really about the narrator's strange nocturnal fantasies that began at home in southern Germany and, in the light of his subsequent meeting with Lolita, seem to have let him glimpse mysterious events from the history of her family, the female line of which is apparently doomed to suffer madness and death shortly after giving birth. The story is essentially a curio, but its rediscovery naturally raised the question of whether or not Nabokov—who actually lived in the same Berlin district as von Eschwege in the mid-1930s—could have read it and been influenced by it, however subliminally. We cannot know—the author himself never mentioned the story but cited quite different inspirations—while Dmitri Nabokov claims any influence is unlikely since his father hardly read German at all at the time. Even so it is eerie to think that Dolores Haze, conceived in Mexico, might have had a spiritual ancestor with Hispanic connections, a woman famous for her reputation for tempting men and someone for whom pregnancy would mean inevitable death.

Hindsight is a fine thing, and it is sometimes possible to see patterns and connections where none exist. The question of what, if anything, Nabokov owed to von Eschwege caused a literary stir when the first *Lolita* was unearthed and subsequently discussed in Michael Marr's book *The Two Lolitas*. Marr, however, concluded that "nothing of what we admire in [Nabokov's] *Lolita* is already to be found in the tale; the former is in no way deducible from the latter."

A more questionable although undeniably fascinating claim of inspiration came from Charlie Chaplin's biographer Joyce Milton, who maintained in her biography *Tramp: The Life of Charlie Chaplin* that Chaplin's 1924 marriage at the age of thirty-five to sixteen-year-old Lillita Grey was Nabokov's real inspiration. The name "Lillita" is certainly a temptation to rush to judgment (after one film appearance as Lillita McMurray, the young actress in question later variously appeared as Lita Grey and Lita Grey Chaplin). She was pregnant by Chaplin when they married in November 1924 and the subsequent child was Charles Chaplin Jr., who, along with his brother Sydney born a year later in 1926, became a bargaining chip in the highly acrimonious divorce that soon followed. It is hard to see any real parallels between Humbert and Chaplin, apart from their shared "Europeanness" and the latter's well-known fondness for very young girls, a tendency that, like Charles Dodgson, he seemed to always find convenient to believe was essentially innocent and nonsexual. Also it would seem that it was only the coincidence of Grey's unusual first name—a lilting variant of Lolita—combined with Chaplin's enormous fame that made her a candidate for Nabokov's muse.

For many years American radio offered a long-running and decidedly ambiguous entertainment featuring a scheming female child who was constantly manipulating her ineffectual father. This was Fanny Brice's slightly creepy creation Baby Snooks, a well-worn vaudeville persona revived for radio's *Good News* show and *Maxwell House Time* before the character became so popular that Brice was finally rewarded, in 1948, with a Snooks radio show of her own. Throughout a long career Baby Snooks had remained of uncertain preschool age; Brice was by now fifty-seven. Alfred Appel Jr. has commented that *The Baby Snooks Show* "explored all but one of the various ways the tyrannical Baby Snooks could victimize her daddy and hold him in her sway." Appel also pointed out that Snooks's daddy (first played by Alan Reed, then Hanley Stafford) was referred to as Daddums, a sobriquet that Humbert twice adopts for comic effect in *Lolita*. Appel's conjecture that Nabokov's invented town of Briceland may be a reference to the famous Ziegfeld girl is, however, probably a case of finding significance where only coincidence exists.

Baby Snooks was a fascinating if slightly disturbing creation that echoed—and ultimately extended—the silent movies' fondness for casting adult young women as very young girls. There is no evidence that Nabokov ever heard any of Fanny Brice's many shows that featured Snooks, although he did vaguely recall the look but not the name of a cartoon strip little girl monster and referenced her in *Lolita*.

Lolita's closest identifiable fictional ancestor possessed no name at all, lilting or otherwise. Her realization was first foreshadowed by an incidental character in Nabokov's novel *Dar* (*The Gift*), completed in 1938. Offering a fanciful synopsis for an unwritten novel, the character in question proposes:

> Imagine this kind of thing: an old dog—but still in his prime, fiery, thirsting for happiness—gets to know a widow, and she has a daughter, still quite a little girl—you know what I mean—when nothing is formed yet, but already she has a way of walking that drives you out of your mind. A slip of a girl, very fair, pale, with blue under the eyes—and of course she doesn't even look at the old goat. What to do? Well, not long thinking, he ups and marries the widow. Okay. They settle down the three of them. Here you can go on indefinitely—the temptation, the eternal torment, the itch, the mad hopes. And the upshot—a miscalculation. Time flies, he gets older, she blossoms out—and not a sausage. Just walks by and scorches you with a look of contempt. Eh? D'you feel here a kind of Dostoevskian tragedy?

Almost immediately after the completion of *Dar*, in Paris in the autumn of 1939, Nabokov wrote his Russian novella *Volshebnik* (*The Enchanter*), which uses the first part of the above narrative premise. Unpublished, the story was assumed lost after Nabokov and his family relocated to the United States in 1940 (in point of fact the author mistakenly recalled destroying it). Unexpectedly, *Volshebnik* resurfaced among some papers in February 1959, and its author, more often than not a man impatient with his own failings as a young artist, found himself not entirely displeased by the rediscovered piece.

"I have reread *Volshebnik* with considerably more pleasure than I experienced when recalling it as a dead scrap during my work on *Lolita*," Nabokov wrote in a letter to the president of publisher G.P. Putnam's Sons, with a view to getting the novella translated into English and finally published. (It was not to appear until 1986, almost a decade after Vladimir Nabokov's death, in a translation by his son, Dmitri.) The original Russian version was at last published in 1991, half a century after it was written. Unlike *Lolita*, *Volshebnik* is easily summarized: A middle-aged pedophile marries an ailing woman in order to be near her twelve-year-old daughter. When the woman finally dies he takes the girl on a vacation, planning to establish a sexual relationship with her over time while dressing up this protracted seduction as a game of make-believe. In their hotel room, however, he is too impatient and fondles her once she goes to sleep. When she awakes and begins screaming, the man knows all is lost and runs panic-stricken from the hotel in suicidal search of "a torrent, a precipice, a railroad track." A thundering, heavy vehicle obligingly supplies the deus ex machina and the story's ending. Compared to the infinitely richer *Lolita*, *Volshebnik* seems a rather mechanical trifle and, although beautifully written and translated, does not make us care much about any of the participants in Nabokov's miniature Dostoevskian tragedy. Only in the occasional fleeting detail does there seem to be any live connecting tissue to *Lolita*, as in the introduction of *Volshebnik*'s nameless nymphet (who incidentally shares Lolita's pale gray eye color) in a park on roller skates. She is "leaning well-forward and rhythmically swinging her relaxed arms," and this activity finds an echo in an early section of *Lolita* where, among the European parade of nymphets who will haunt Humbert with their incendiary multiple presences, there is a beautiful child in a tartan frock, who clunks her wheel-clad foot near to him on a bench, leaning against him for support while she tightens the strap on her roller skate. Lolita bears a small scar on her calf acquired from a roller skate.

It is with something of a jolt that we see this line of Lolita's predecessors emerging from the past—abused little girls both real and invented but all inevitably distanced by intervening time and the context of the day—and suddenly starting to catch up with the novel and snag in its fabric. Many readers of *Lolita* understandably miss the significance of a certain real-life crime entirely, for Humbert refers to it directly only once toward the end of the book when he returns to the town of Ramsdale with murder in his heart. It is five years after he left the town to take possession of orphaned Lolita; back once more and sitting in a downtown hotel bar, he is recognized by one Mrs. Chatfield, a local resident with a good memory for faces. Chatfield's chattiness fails to disguise her sharp curiosity, and this prompts Humbert, now past caring since he knows his life is heading for ruin, to wonder idly if she thinks that he did to Lolita what fifty-year-old Frank LaSalle did to Sally Horner in 1948. The throwaway reference is to a haunting real-life case that received little mainstream news coverage at the time, only finally coming to public attention in March 1950 when a number of unsigned reports from international press agencies started to appear in American newspapers. The following is one of them and comes from the Associated Press:

SAN JOSE, Calif., March 22—(AP)—A plump little girl of 13 told police today she accompanied a 52-year-old man on a two-year tour of the country, in fear he would expose her as a shop-lifter.

The girl, Florence Sally Horner of Camden, N.J., was found here last night after she appealed to Eastern relatives "send the FBI for me, please?"

Her companion, Frank La Salle, an unemployed mechanic, was said by County Prosecutor Michael H. Cohen in Camden to be under indictment for her abduction.

Officers said the girl told them La Salle had forced her to submit to sexual relations.

The nice looking youngster, with light brown hair and blue-green eyes, attributed her troubles to a Club she joined in a Camden school. One of the requirements, she said, was that each member steal something from a ten-cent store.

She stole an article, she related, and La Salle happened to be watching her. She said he told her he was an FBI Agent; that "We have a place for girls like you."

Sally said she went away with him, under his threat that unless she did, he would have her placed in a reform school.

Humbert too threatened his young prisoner stepdaughter with reformatory or some form of juvenile detention home if he were ever arrested. In a sly feat of authorial misdirection (this time Nabokov's), Humbert, in 1947, browbeats Lolita by referring to a "recent" newspaper report concerning a middle-aged morals offender who violated the Mann Act by transporting a nine-year-old girl across state lines for immoral purposes. Humbert says pointedly that she, Lolita, is not nine but nearly thirteen and should not consider herself his "cross-country slave." This admonitory speech clearly draws on an actual phrase in one of the newspaper reports of the LaSalle case that did not appear until 1950. In 1947, Sally Horner—then not quite as young as nine but certainly younger than the age cited in the future news reports—had as yet not even been abducted. This very knowing device by Nabokov confirms to future literalists not only that he knew the details of the LaSalle case perfectly well but that he was also aware that he was citing them out of chronological sequence. Nabokov uses an even more devious documentary device when he has Humbert refer to and relate another true-life crime of the day, that of G. Edward Grammar, a thirty-five-year-old New York office manager arraigned for murdering his wife and trying to make her death look like a car accident. Nabokov uses an actual 1952 Associated Press report published in the *New York Times* under the headline "Charge Is Due Today in 'Perfect Murder'" and embellishes it with numerous Humbertian flourishes. Accordingly the press report sentence "The wheels were still spinning when the officers removed Mrs. G's body" becomes "The wheels were still *gently* spinning *in the mellow sunlight* when the officers removed Mrs. G's body." All of which shows how *Lolita* is shot through with the kind of authenticity that does not depend upon stark, spare, newsroom prose for its effect but rather on how Humbert's fantasy world and the "real" world run parallel, occasionally overlapping and clashing until eventually the fantasy runs out. In the instance of the Sally Horner case Nabokov borrowed heavily and without concealment from the real-life abduction. ("A creative writer," Nabokov wrote in his own memoir, *Strong Opinions*, "must study carefully the works of his rivals, including the Almighty.")

Florence Sally Horner was, like Lolita, fatherless. Also like Lolita she underwent a protracted car ride across America with an abductor who used her sexually while keeping her in line with threats of incarceration (for Sally, life on the road lasted twenty-one months, almost twice Lolita's sentence). Finally, just like Lolita, Sally eventually managed to effect her own escape, although not by means of any dramatic act: she simply phoned a sister back east, asking her to tell the authorities to pick her up in a San Jose auto court. Automobiles, it turned out, were clearly bad news in the short, sad life of Sally Horner, because less than two years after her liberation from Frank LaSalle's mobile prison, she was killed in an unrelated road accident. Nabokov knew this too, copying out by hand a shortened version of a newspaper report on her death dated August 20, 1952:

> Woodbine, N.Y. — Sally Horner, 15-year-old Camden, N.J., girl who spent 21 months as the captive of a middle-aged morals offender a few years ago, was killed in a highway mishap early Monday. . . . Sally vanished from her Camden home in 1948 and wasn't heard from again until 1950 when she told a harrowing story of spending 21 months as the cross-country slave of Frank LaSalle, 52.
>
> LaSalle, a mechanic, was arrested in San Jose, Calif. . . . He pleaded guilty to charges of kidnapping and was sentenced to 30 to 35 years in prison. He was branded a "moral leper" by the sentencing judge.

In the foreword to Humbert's memoir, his fictional editor, John Ray Jr., refers to its author as an outstanding example of moral leprosy.

So Sally Horner's case brought the twentieth-century casebook history of real-life pedophilia up-to-date with the time frame of Lolita, even overtaking the action by a couple of years. In the handful of news photos that appeared in 1950, Sally, freed from temporary protective custody and about to embark on what she could hardly know would be the final twenty or so months of her life, looks unexceptional. Her broad, pleasant, but unremarkable face was usually shown in a snapshot laid adjacent to a harsher shot of the drawn and hawkish Frank LaSalle, now imprisoned effectively for life. Interestingly, no one subsequently thought to cast her as a temptress.

If Sally was one of Lolita's contemporaneous soul mates, she was of course also just the latest name in an endless line of hapless abductees that extends beyond the novel and on into the cheerless future. The world's news media still intermittently highlight certain such cases. A ten-year-old Japanese girl, Fusako Sano, was kidnapped and held captive by Nobuyuki Sato for nine years, from 1990 to 2000. Teenager Tanya Kach, of Pittsburgh, Pennsylvania, was confined against her will at the home of thirty-seven-year-old Thomas Hose from 1996 to 2006. There have been more—the cases of Polly Klaas, Elizabeth Smart, and JonBenet Ramsey will be discussed later in the context of what the newspapers made of them— and there will be more still, random and sad examples of fantasies made real and young lives derailed. One particular case from the present century is worth special mention since it sprouts enough dark coincidences to make the late Vladimir Nabokov, wherever he might now reside, smile once again at the extraordinary patterns of chance and mimicry that occur in real, chaotic life as well as in carefully structured art.

Natascha Kampusch, born in 1988 in Austria, grew up fatherless like Lolita even though her mother, Brigitta Sirny, did enjoy a fairly stable relationship with another man. When Natascha was ten she was abducted while walking to school alone after an argument with her mother (shades of Charlotte Haze's daily domestic battles with her daughter). Her abductor, Wolfgang Priklopil, imprisoned her in a small, secretly constructed room in his house for most of the eight years of her confinement. Although she refused to discuss "personal or intimate details" after she finally escaped in 2006, the tacit assumption is that Priklopil used her as a sex slave, and Kampusch did admit to a media advisor, although not in front of the TV cameras (hers was a very structured reintroduction to society), that Priklopil beat her badly from time to time. Perhaps of particular interest to those unimaginative souls who persist in seeing Lolita's dull cooperation with Humbert's exploitative regime as complicity pure and simple is the fact that Priklopil once took his prisoner on a skiing holiday in Vienna and would even take her shopping occasionally. The complexities of their enforced relationship are still not fully explained and may eventually yield some awkward truths, but in 2006 the case provided an eerie echo of both Sally and Lolita, neither of whom could ever have been guarded night and day, every day, but both of whom somehow lacked the spur or spirit to escape their captors until much later than they might have been expected to do. This phenomenon now has a name, courtesy of a 1973 bank siege at Norrmalmstorg, Stockholm, Sweden, in which the robbers held employees hostage from August 23 to August 28. "Stockholm syndrome" is the phrase that describes what happens when, defying all conventional logic, victims became emotionally attached to their victimizers. Wolfgang Priklopil himself was never available for comment since, like the pedophile in *Volshebnik*, once his captive successfully escaped and eventually raised the alarm (Natascha Kampusch's wild escape through suburban gardens and streets, during which she completely failed to interest anyone she met in her plight, has itself a dark Nabokovian tinge of farce) he immediately sought his personal "torrent . . . precipice . . . railroad track." For him it was not to be the wheels of a thundering truck, as in *Volshebnik*, but those of a suburban train approaching Vienna's Wien Nord station. The outcome was the same.

[3]

A VERY 1950S SCANDAL:
Hurricane Lolita

THE INTERMITTENT SCANDALS THAT DOTTED THE AMERICAN LITerary landscape from the 1930s onward were characterized by a randomness born of uncertainty. There were no written rules (at least none that were not susceptible to very variable legal interpretation), just vague boundaries of "decency" that might be tested by sensationalists or artists. That atmosphere of uncertainty favored the forces of conservatism, and so the unwritten nature of what constituted obscenity might be seen as a weapon of restraint in itself. For a time, however, twentieth-century America did have a written moral code, and although it was intended to control only the movies, it reflected much broader establishment concerns about the general threats posed by artists to society in general. It was the Motion Picture Production Code of 1930, better known as the Hays Code, named for ex-Republican politician and ex-postmaster general Will H. Hays, who was appointed the first president of the Motion Picture Producers and Distributors Association and therefore became the nominal father of the code. The Hays Code was bold enough to set down its guidelines and exclusion zones in full literal foolishness. Although it was in operation for only thirty years or so, the code neatly set out the establishment view of what was thought admissible to depict—at least on the screen—during the period leading up to and beyond the time of Lolita's publication. It began unpromisingly enough: "Though regarding motion pictures primarily as entertainment without any explicit purpose of teaching or propaganda, [producers] know that the motion picture within its own field of entertainment may be directly responsible for spiritual or moral progress, for higher types of social life, and for much correct thinking."

Sex for the fun of it, it seems, had no place in correct thinking: "The sanctity of the institution of marriage and the home shall be upheld. Pictures shall not infer that low forms of sex relationship are the accepted or common thing." It was an unambiguous instruction that was elaborately expanded into specific areas of moral concern. "Sex perversion or any inference to it is forbidden," it states. "Miscegenation (sex relationships between the white and black races) is forbidden." "Children's sex organs are never to be exposed." There was a great deal more along the same lines, amounting to a directive not just for making movies but for making movies into instruments of a moral education program for adults. The code also identified what it saw as the distinction between fit topics for books and fit topics for films. "A book describes; a film vividly presents," is stated confidently. "One presents on a cold page; the other by apparently living people."

His photographs identify Will H. Hays as an apparently living person (even though some of his sterner official portraits have a rather postmortem look to them). He was, shall we say, an unphotogenic man in possession of jug ears and a jagged smirk that perhaps made him an unfortunate standard-bearer for wholesome American values. (His moral reign, however, happened at a time when image was deemed less important than it is now; one parenthetically wonders whether saturnine fifties TV personality Ed Sullivan would even get a job reading the local news in front of today's cameras.) So Hays became the unlovely and unloved poster boy of a notorious code that was often booed when a summary of its principles appeared on the movie screen prior to the feature film—hardly the sign of a regulatory body in touch with the public.

The code was right about one thing, however: books, for whatever reason, were indeed somewhat ahead of movies in the frankness stakes, even if James Joyce's *Ulysses* (1922) did run into censorship trouble in the United States during its prepublication serialization in *The Little Review* magazine. The finished novel was duly banned from U.S. publication until the 1930s, when Random House finally engineered the importation of a French edition with the full knowledge that it would be seized by customs. It was, and the ensuing trial—*United States v. One Book Called Ulysses*—resulted in U.S. District Judge John M. Woolsey ruling that the book was not pornographic and so could not be classed as obscene. In fact, *Ulysses*'s only transgression in the eyes of the prudish was that it made passing mention—in the course of a massive, elaborate, allusive narrative—of masturbation, sexual intercourse, defecation, urination, and orgasm. Not particularly obsessed with corporeality, Joyce's novel simply avoided omitting it.

It had taken well over a decade to get *Ulysses* into the United States, and the protracted case had surely been complicated by Joyce's wildly allusive and often challenging style. Like *Lolita*, it too was, in the derisory phrase of Alfred Appel's army colleague, "Goddamn Litachure."

Scandalous writing of a less high-flown sort next tested the would-be book banners and came in the shape of Kathleen Winsor's proto-bodice-ripper *Forever Amber* (1944), which immediately stimulated a popular appetite for erotic fiction. Her impressively researched book was set in Restoration England and concerned a female social climber with a pragmatic moral sense and an eye on bedding the king; it triggered several charges of pornography and calls for bans across America. The Massachusetts attorney general found in it seventy instances of sexual intercourse, thirty-nine illegitimate pregnancies, seven abortions, ten descriptions of women undressing in front of men, and many "miscellaneous objectionable passages," and so prosecuted.

In the case *Attorney General v. Book Named Forever Amber* the Massachusetts Supreme Court eventually concluded that Winsor's historical research was thorough and resulted in an honest portrayal of the mores of the time and place in which the book was set. Then, with the kind of wit conspicuous by its absence in the world of Will H. Hays, the court decided against banning *Forever Amber* because its wealth of sexual escapades acted as "a soporific rather than an aphrodisiac" and "that while the novel was conducive to sleep, it was not conducive to a desire to sleep with a member of the opposite sex."

In 1946, literary critic Edmund Wilson published his second book of fiction, *Memoirs of Hecate County*. Wilson was at the time a friend and supporter of Vladimir Nabokov, although eventually the two men of letters would fall out, partly over Wilson's low opinion of *Lolita*. Published by Doubleday, *Memoirs of Hecate County* received good reviews and sold almost sixty thousand copies before the Society for the Suppression of Vice brought suit against the publisher in July 1946, on the grounds of objecting to a number of frank but otherwise unexceptionable heterosexual sex scenes. As a result, in November of that year the Court of Special Sessions of New York found against Doubleday, an outcome that was upheld in two appeals.

It took until 1948 for the Supreme Court to make a mockery of justice, when a ninth judge, whose decision would have broken the four-to-four deadlock reached by the other eight, disqualified himself by having talked to Wilson about the book. This left the New York Court of Appeals decision in effect. Banned in New York, where its publisher was based, *Memoirs of Hecate County* ceased to be sold throughout the United States.

Throughout much of the 1950s Wilson's now effectively banned book became the focus of numerous absurd legal complications, including tentative imports of a version published in Britain that served to make it available from compliant bookstores to those who really wanted it. In relation to *Lolita*, however, the fortunes of Wilson's book provided a protracted and discouraging precedent to Nabokov's potential U.S. publishers in the 1950s.

If fewer members of the general public read the next literary bombshell to hit America's homespun values, it was not due to suppression but to the nature of the work. The Kinsey Reports were published five years apart and were heavyweight academic tomes that found a popular audience mainly through sensational sound bites, often misquoted and sometimes invented. *Sexual Behavior in the Human Male* (1948) and *Sexual Behavior in the Human Female* (1953), by Indiana University zoologist Dr. Alfred C. Kinsey, were presented as dispassionate and clinical books based upon many hundreds of coded interviews with American men and women. Will H. Hays, who died in 1954, might well have entered his grave already spinning after learning that according to Kinsey and his team at their Institute of Sexual Research, sexual orientation was a far more complex issue than *The Adventures of Ozzie and Harriet* might have Middle America believe.

Kinsey's reports noted that 45 percent of male subjects had reacted sexually to persons of both genders in the course of their adult lives, 50 percent of married men had experienced extramarital sex during marriage, erotic responses to sadomasochistic stories were recorded in 22 percent of men and 12 percent of women, and the frequency of sexual intercourse within marriage had been clocked with scientific precision by Kinsey's team (data provided by women indicated 2.8 times a week in late teens, 2.2 times a week by age thirty, and 1.0 times a week by age fifty). In addition to interviews, Kinsey's sources included the diaries of convicted child molesters, something that led to many attempts to discredit Kinsey personally by arguing that some of his very precise data about the sexual experiences of young children could only have been gained by illegal participation and direct observation. Whatever the validity of Kinsey's methods and statistics—and these were certainly controversial—the very fact that such taboos were being discussed openly seemed to cause as much outrage as the findings they unearthed. Surely America did not behave like this behind closed doors—and if it did, surely no one should ever talk about it so frankly.

The next popular fiction scandal would also hit close to home. *Peyton Place*, Grace Metalious's 1956 exposé of the sordid secrets of a fictional New England town, enjoyed a commercial success comparable only to that of Margaret Mitchell's *Gone with the Wind* (1936), selling sixty thousand copies within the first ten days. With its lively litany of social injustice, murder, adultery, and abortion, *Peyton Place* would remain on the *New York Times*' bestseller list for over a year and seemed to mark an emphatic rejection of any hopes of art encouraging "correct thinking." One episode in Metalious's novel originally had a character named Selena Cross murder her father because he had been sexually abusing her for years. The real-life inspiration was twenty-year-old Jane Glenn, a New Hampshire girl who, in 1947, confessed to the same crime—and to burying the corpse beneath a sheep pen with the help of her younger brother. Metalious's editor changed Selena Cross's victim to stepfather, feeling that murder was acceptable but incest was a vice too far. This assumption finds an echo in Humbert's own moral prioritizing when he notes from his prison cell that, sitting in judgment on himself, he would dismiss the murder charge and give himself at least thirty years for rape.

Before the American public would be allowed to read these words and the rest of *Lolita*, Nabokov's book would have to make its way through a maze of obstacles. When it had done so, it unleashed a scandal to overshadow all of its recent predecessors. Since it involved scholarly, retiring fifty-nine-year-old Vladimir Nabokov (a man whose substantial body of fiction contained no obscene words and bore eloquent testimony to his total indifference toward books with social or moral messages), it was somehow fitting that this chronicler of unexpected coincidences and unintended consequences should find himself at the center of an international uproar about morality, social responsibility, and obscenity. Nabokov had placed at the heart of his greatest novel something that Joyce had not touched upon and Hays had not even dared to articulate in order to forbid: pedophilia.

The journey toward scandal was slow and complex. *Lolita*'s first publishing house, the Paris-based Olympia Press, had been inherited by Maurice Girodias from his father, who had published Henry Miller's *Tropic of Cancer* and *Tropic of Capricorn* in the 1930s. Girodias junior, falling on hard times in 1953, resolved to make money by publishing, in English, every book he could acquire that had fallen foul of Anglo-American censorship. The censor's thumbs down was his only criterion; good, bad, or indifferent, if it had been banned, Girodias wanted it. To be fair, Girodias had also published some respectable authors (including Lawrence Durrell, J. P. Donleavy, and Samuel Beckett) and at least one notable piece of erotica, *L'histoire d'O* by Anne Desclos (who wrote such books either anonymously or pseudonymously as Pauline Réage while enjoying rather a good reputation under another literary pseudonym, Dominique Aury). Nabokov, however, knew little of Girodias and was guided by his French agent and friends in Paris. Since Girodias had until recently owned another imprint, a prestigious art book subsidiary called Editions du Chêne, this further seemed to enhance his reputation as a serious publisher. So when he offered to publish *Lolita*, Nabokov (who had already had the novel rejected by Viking, dubbed "pure pornography" by Simon & Schuster, and further rejected by three more American publishers) jumped at the chance. It proved a hasty leap. *Lolita* came out in September 1955 in Paris, in Olympia's Traveler's Edition, a format aimed at the English-speaking tourist trade and comprising mainly pornographic titles. Copyright had been assigned jointly to Nabokov and Olympia Press.

The final three months of 1955 were stressful for the author, who, having just recovered from a serious bout of lumbago, was now having difficulty finding a publisher for his next novel, *Pnin* (or *My Poor Pnin* as it was titled at the time). One of Nabokov's most dependable editors, Katharine White at *The New Yorker* magazine, had just left the editorial department, and the year looked to be drawing to a rather unsatisfactory close when Nabokov received an unexpected Christmas present. It came from a writer who, two decades earlier, had been sued for writing a film review suggesting that nine-year-old Shirley Temple's coquettish appeal to middle-aged men was a very calculated sexual effect.

The British *Sunday Times* Christmas issue for 1955 invited various people to choose their favorite books of the year. One of the selectors, Graham Greene, was already well known as the author of *The Power and the Glory* (1940), *The Heart of the Matter* (1948), and *The End of the Affair* (1951). He nominated *Lolita* as one of the best three books of the year. It was a modest but valuable accolade, although one that was to lead to a furor and bring Nabokov a level of notoriety that he could never have anticipated. The outrage began not in the United States but in Britain.

Sixty-eight-year-old John Gordon was chief editor of the British newspaper the *Sunday Express*, a paper that, by the standards of the day, pitched frequently sensational stories to a "respectable" British readership that might balk at buying the more nakedly sensational scandal sheet, the *News of the World*. On reading Greene's review Gordon sent to Paris for a copy of *Lolita*, which he immediately pronounced "about the filthiest book I've ever read." Gordon went on to predict that "anyone who published it or sold it here would certainly go to prison." Despite similar reactions by various other British publishers, the relatively new publishing house of Weidenfeld & Nicolson quickly accepted it but elected to postpone publishing until an imminent government proposal for revision of Britain's nebulous law on pornography was accepted or rejected; a bill had been submitted to Parliament the previous year and was making slow progress. The hoped-for revision would mean that a book could only be prosecuted if it were to be judged obscene as a whole; selected passages would not be sufficient to prompt seizure of books or the prosecution of booksellers on the whim of the police, which was the prevailing state of affairs. A proper discussion of literary merit with expert witnesses would have to take place in court, and Weidenfeld & Nicolson believed *Lolita* could be vindicated that way if it came to it.

Meanwhile, a full-blown quarrel between Greene and Gordon had erupted and was reported in the *New York Times Book Review* along with comments from many supporters of *Lolita*. Galvanized by the controversy, American publishers at last started making Nabokov offers for the U.S. rights to *Lolita*. On two occasions—in June and November 1956—U.S. customs seized and then released imported copies of the Olympia edition. In December of the same year the French Ministère de l'Intérieur banned twenty-five English-language Olympia titles, *Lolita* among them. This was in reality a devious political move initiated by the British Home Office, concerned that British tourists were bringing copies of *Lolita* back into the country now that John Gordon had raised the book's profile with his condemnation; the other twenty-four books affected were simply camouflage for the real objective. The French complied mainly because a major international incident, the Suez Crisis, had for once made Britain and France cooperative peacetime neighbors. The French press was immediately up in arms at what it saw as a betrayal of France's traditional cultural freedom; it identified Nabokov's book as the true cause of the blanket ban and, by January 1957, had elevated the legal dispute into "l'affaire Lolita." With this press support, Maurice Girodias sued to have the ban lifted; he finally triumphed in January 1958. France's highly regarded publishing house Gallimard arranged to publish a French-language edition, which would be very well received—a particular fan was Raymond Queneau, a longtime Gallimard employee whose own linguistically playful novel *Zazie dans le métro* (1959) would transpose something of Lolita's nymphet feistiness to another little girl, this time in a Parisian setting.

Across the Atlantic, some of the difficulties that were delaying *Lolita*'s American publication were due to Girodias's insistence of taking an absurdly large slice of the action (two publishers withdrew their offers when he demanded up to 62.5 percent of Nabokov's royalties) as well as his fitful bids to flood the American black market with the Olympia edition, something that risked negating the book's copyright in the United States. But the major obstacle remained the very real fear of prosecution. The last man standing in all the U.S. bidding and withdrawing was Walter Minton of G.P. Putnam's Sons. The book had come to his notice rather late, but, despite all the problems, he wanted it. Minton suggested a pragmatic approach toward Girodias and a muscular one toward the threat of prosecution. He could not guarantee to defend *Lolita* all the way to the Supreme Court, but he would do everything else to reduce the chance of prosecution. On publication day (August 18, 1958) the *New York Times*' daily reviewer, Orville Prescott, dismissed *Lolita* as highbrow pornography, but most other reviews were favorable, notably Elizabeth Janeway's intelligent and sensitive appraisal in the same paper's Sunday *Book Review*, published a day earlier.

Lolita took off, selling one hundred thousand copies in three weeks. When Putnam's took out an ad in the *New York Times Book Review* of August 21, there was no shortage of rave reviews to cite. Graham Greene, William Styron, and Lionel Trilling all praised it fulsomely, and even Dorothy Parker seemed to acknowledge that for once her tendency to deploy her vitriolic wit even when reviewing things she liked had no place here. "A fine book, a distinguished book—all right, then—a great book," she wrote.

Lolita was then a huge, immediate success, although Nabokov, who always maintained a remarkable workload, had done a lot of other things, both literary and academic, since writing it and now, at the time of its successful publication, was completely absorbed by the task of writing a short story about a butterfly. "V. serenely indifferent" was Véra Nabokov's diary entry about her husband's reaction to finally hitting the commercial jackpot after a lifetime of poorly paid literary toil.

Lolita was never prosecuted in the United States, a source of great satisfaction to Nabokov, who passionately loved his adopted homeland. Ironically, the many delays to publication had probably helped matters since the incremental efforts of many liberal-minded publishers had recently contributed to a more mature climate surrounding literary censorship. What resistance there was, predictably enough, had the opposite effect to that which had been intended. As soon as the Cincinnati Public Library banned it, *Lolita* immediately reached the top of the bestsellers list. When the Los Angeles Public Library was "exposed" for circulating a copy, the only result was a boom in sales of the book in California. The Texas town of Lolita gravely debated whether it should change its name to Jackson, presumably in case it was mistaken for a little girl. But the feared American obscenity trial never took place—at least not in a courtroom. Instead the book became the butt of endless jokes and cartoons. Again America was absorbing something controversial into its popular culture instead of subjecting it to a witch hunt. Mainstream comedians all had a *Lolita* gag, the unspoken basis of the joke being that *Lolita* was a dirty book. Milton Berle, Bob Hope, Steve Allen, Dean Martin, and the rest all cracked wise, although only Groucho Marx's parodic gag wears well: "I've put off reading *Lolita* for six years, till she's eighteen." Steve Allen had mounted a comedy skit that featured Lolita and Zorro, and Milton Berle's first show of 1959 began with Uncle Miltie offering his congratulations to Lolita because "she is thirteen now." Dean Martin claimed that as a non-gambler in Las Vegas he had nothing to do but sit in his hotel lobby and read children's books—*The Bobbsey Twins. Pollyanna. Lolita.*

All this playfulness marked the beginning of Lolita Haze's disparagement; the advance guard of what would prove to be a legion of faux Lolitas would soon start to emerge. Perhaps the very first was the ponytailed little girl who, incredibly, on Halloween came to the Nabokovs' door looking for treats while dressed (by her parents!) as Lolita; the famous name was spelled out on a sign she bore and—even more sinister, since it betrayed a detailed knowledge of the book—she carried a tennis racket. Nabokov was quite shocked. If only he had known what lay in store for his nymphet.

In Europe—and even in Australia—the Lolita disputes rumbled on, often with a kind of weird totalitarian logic. France's Conseil d'État had reinstated the overturned ban on the Olympia edition. In the UK, a new Obscene Publications Bill was presented to Parliament and seemed now to hinge on *Lolita*, prompting a letter of support for the book to be sent to the the *Times* of London and bearing the signatures of twenty-one more or less distinguished authors. Critic Bernard Levin wrote a superb defense of the novel for *The*

Spectator, a venerable British weekly magazine with a lively conservative agenda. The political infighting made life difficult for Nigel Nicolson, one-half of Weidenfeld & Nicolson, who also happened to be a Member of Parliament representing the genteel south coast English resort of Bournemouth. His firm had still not published the book but would eventually do so on November 6, 1959. It sold out immediately and made the fortune of a publishing house that, over the next thirty years, was to publish in Britain everything of Nabokov's that it possibly could, making George Weidenfeld and Vladimir Nabokov mutual admirers. On the other side of the world in New South Wales, police raided the offices of the *Sydney Nation*, believing an illegal copy of *Lolita* must be there as the paper had just printed an extract from the novel; they found nothing.

The complex literary and legal ruckus surrounding *Lolita* would gradually subside, but the next *Lolita* scandal was already in the making. Nabokov had sold the film rights of his book to James B. Harris and Stanley Kubrick, so now Lolita Haze and Humbert Humbert were about to make the fraught transition from what Hays had called "the cold page" to embodiment by "apparently living people." For a middle-aged actor to impersonate Humbert might be seen as no more than a risky professional challenge, but for a prepubescent girl to embody Lolita on-screen looked like a decidedly dangerous prospect. We may charitably assume that Nabokov's otherwise absurd suggestion that a "dwarfess" be hired to play Lolita was simply a comment designed to avert any charge of being implicated in the corrupting of a living, breathing child. He had no need to worry; others would take care of the corrupting. They had been doing it in Hollywood for years.

[4]

LOLITA IN MOVIELAND 1:
Little Victims and Little Princesses

WHEN LOLITA ACHIEVED WIDESPREAD FAME IN THE MIDDLE OF
the twentieth century, it suddenly became retrospectively clear that
her predecessors had been a staple of Hollywood films stretching
back to the earliest days of the medium. Certainly if a "Lolita" was
a defenseless child who exerted unconscious sexual pressure on a
certain type of middle-aged man, then she was nothing new, just
something newly christened. In an interesting example of a label
being applied retrospectively as well as prospectively, little Lolitas
could suddenly be identified popping up all over the place in the
silent movie parade of fetching and often symbolically disabled
little girls. Orphaned, crippled, blind, or—if they were lucky—just
vaguely undernourished, these pioneer nymphets had been subjected to an extraordinary amount of mature male adoration (and
physical threats) in movies that seemed to pick up where Charles
Dickens's novels had left off. As with Dickens's Little Nell, Little
Emily, and Little Dorrit, that emotionally loaded word "little" was

to feature frequently in the promotional screen name of many a child actress (Little Mary Pickford and Little Blanche Sweet, for example), as well as in the titles of their films (*The Little Princess, Little Annie Rooney, The Poor Little Rich Girl*, and so on). Usually helming these enterprises and guiding their young stars' careers were forty-something men about whose sexual inclinations we are entitled to wonder.

David Lewelyn Wark Griffith was already a paternal figure for the medium he helped pioneer ("D. W. Griffith, The Father of Film" was a common rubric), siring literally hundreds of movies. His first was titled *The Adventures of Dollie* (1908), a satisfying coincidence since Dolly was Dolores Haze's school nickname. Griffith was a doting but strict father figure to the very young and usually very submissive actresses he cast and around whom his plots often revolved. A young D. W. Griffith heroine stood a pretty good chance of being alternately worshipped by the camera and subjected to what can sometimes look like startling bouts of sexual sadism. Although the innocent heroine threatened by sex and violence was a common enough plot cliché of the Victorian melodrama, it is not only today's sensibilities that find Griffith's films particularly egregious in this respect; it was pointed out as long ago as 1920, in the movie magazine *Photoplay*, that the father of film seemed to have an "obsession with scenes in which women and girls are beaten or attacked." Griffith's ambivalent girl-child preoccupations seemed to find their fullest expression in his film version of a Thomas Burke story taken from a collection of pieces titled *Limehouse Nights*. Here racism and child abuse came together in one unsettling package: *Broken Blossoms; or, The Yellow Man and the Girl* (1919). Its heroine, twelve-year-old Lucy Burrows (valiantly embodied by twenty-six-year-old Lillian Gish), is a doll-hugging child who suffers routine beatings from her adoptive prizefighter father until she is rescued by Chinese immigrant Cheng Huan. The depiction of her savior's contained lust for her results in a strange prefiguring of Humbert's early days in the Haze household, where he can only watch and long for Lolita as she goes about her desultory daily routine, unaware of her extraordinary nymphet power.

Griffith's fondness for playing the little-girl-in-distress card so relentlessly throughout his long career may or may not have been a playing out of his private sexual behavior. He certainly took actress Carol Dempster as his mistress when she was seventeen or younger, but with no corroboration of any sexual relations with underage girls, the question remains unanswered; Griffith may have been entirely innocent or simply too powerful to expose. As in the case of Alfred Hitchcock's well-known obsessive tendency to put his ice-cool blonde heroines through the physical or emotional mill, it could be that Griffith's fixation was nothing more than the public sublimation of dark fantasy. He is now best remembered for directing the sprawling epics *Birth of a Nation* (1915) and *Intolerance* (1916), but Griffith also has the distinction of giving the movies their first recognizable prototype nymphet. To be sure, his version was a composite model, most often portrayed by Lillian Gish and later played by actresses like Carol Dempster, Colleen Moore, and Mae Marsh, but it had been Griffith's idea to create the character in the first place. He was certainly not alone in his interests.

Even a casual semiotic reading of the films of Erich von Stroheim reveals a similar tendency to make his young girls run a gauntlet of lust and retribution. Although he was known to have complained that in most early Hollywood films the heroines were "eternal virgins" rather than real women, Stroheim did not seem reluctant to perpetuate the myth and cleave to the Victorian principle of celebrating innocence found in the gutter and then testing it. He did, however, ring some very bizarre variations on the theme.

Austrian Erich Oswald Stroheim (the "von" was a Hollywood affectation) was most famous as a screen villain ("The Man You

Love to Hate") but turned his hand to directing and writing as well, in some films fulfilling all three roles. He favored plots that involved Don Juan leads and sophisticated romantic complications, and as often as not a young girl would feature somewhere in the sexual melee. In his *Foolish Wives* (1922), Stroheim's character fakes love in order to try to seduce his maid, an ambassador's wife, and a simpleminded fourteen-year-old girl (reenter the damaged little girl stereotype). An uncredited Stroheim wrote *Merry-Go-Round* (1922), a movie in which a roguish count falls in love with a virginal young fairground girl who is also lusted after (and physically threatened) by her boss as well as being chased by a third man who is somewhat surreally accompanied by an orangutan. Strange as it may sound, *Merry-Go-Round* seemed almost conventional compared with Stroheim's *Greed* (1924), a huge, nymphet-free but unwieldy morality tale about gold mining, dentistry, and, well, greed. He was the director this time, and *Greed* served to alienate him from the studios and many audiences with its epic length; a trimmed-down version weighed in at four hours, at the end of which *Greed* concluded that the love of money was the root of all evil. After the film's rocky reception, money was certainly in short supply, especially when Stroheim decided to make what would be far and away his strangest film, *Queen Kelly* (1929). This eccentric project was mainly funded by its star, Gloria Swanson, and cowritten and directed by Stroheim himself. Swanson's lover, Joseph P. Kennedy, was the one who had really put up the money, as a vanity project for her (no doubt the Irish-sounding title also helped), and the result is a chaotic film that gives full rein to Stroheim's fascination with little girls as well as his tendency to let his considerable imagination run riot and hang the expense. Set in a Ruritanian kingdom, it begins with the hero Prince Wolfram (Walter Byron) encountering a whole bevy of orphaned young girls from the local convent while out riding in the country. Irish kid Kitty Kelly (Gloria Swanson) is the one who makes the biggest impression on him after her bloomers fall down and she angrily flings them at him when he laughs at her plight. Smitten by her feisty response to defective underwear, Wolfram subsequently kidnaps Kitty from the convent after staging a diversionary fire and takes her to the royal palace where he seduces her. The villainous Queen Regina V (Seena Owen), who has other marriage plans for Wolfram, is less than welcoming when she discovers the convent girl in the palace and responds by horsewhipping her and imprisoning the prince. Director Stroheim has by now apparently lost all restraint, so it comes as no surprise to discover that Kitty Kelly next inherits a brothel in German East Africa, which opens up a new and unexpected career opportunity for her. The plot becomes even stranger, now with overtones of de Sade, by staging a grotesquely inappropriate marriage for the heroine. From this point, most of the footage is lost and we have only fragments and written intentions to go on, but *Queen Kelly* as it stands, at about seventy minutes, is a hoot, dripping with illicit sexual passion symbolically represented by smoke, fire, and a wealth of phallic candles. At one point Wolfram presses Kitty's bloomers to his lips in a gesture at once romantic and unsettling. Stroheim directed like a man who knew that this might be his last film, and at one point Gloria Swanson had to cable Joe Kennedy, begging him to come and stop the "madman" who was blowing the budget. Needless to say, Kennedy's financial investment in the movie did not pay off, although it did allow his thirty-two-year-old mistress to play convent girl Kelly, a lead part for which she was clearly far too old.

— — —

Charlie Chaplin was far and away the most high-profile member of the early Hollywood set to be obsessed by what were not yet called nymphets. For a time he was indisputably the most famous man in the world, and his fondness for making sentimental slapstick comedies that revolved around very young girls—prostitutes, flower girls, orphans—unquestionably reflected a deeply entrenched personal preference. Prior to his solo movie career, when he was still working with showman and impresario Fred Karno, Chaplin had been smitten with a fifteen-year-old girl called Hetty Kelly, who promptly rejected him. When he saw her one year later, he "was disappointed to notice that she had developed breasts, which he did not find attractive," according to Joyce Milton's 1996 Chaplin biography *Tramp*. At a single stroke, Chaplin seems to have encountered his Annabel Leigh and discovered what Humbert already knew—that nymphets have a very short shelf life before they turn into conventional young women. Next Chaplin developed a crush on twelve-year-old Maybelle Fournier, explaining that "I have always been in love with young girls, not in an amorous way. . . . I just loved to caress and fondle [Maybelle]—not passionately—just to have her in my arms." Actress Mildred Harris was fourteen when Chaplin met her and sixteen when it became clear that she had been caressed and fondled into a pregnancy by him. A Mexican marriage and a prompt divorce ensued. Lillita Grey was barely fifteen when thirty-five-year-old Chaplin first got her pregnant, but even then few outside of Hollywood knew or cared about the recurring link between the artist and his art. That would take an extraordinarily acrimonious marriage during which Lillita's mother (a daunting stage mom) kept a written record of every scurrilous sexual detail of the latest Chaplin ménage, details that would eventually be used in court. Finally, when the inevitable divorce came, the previously tolerant media at last gave the Chaplin child-molesting story full rein. The ensuing scandal was huge but in the end only dented Chaplin's popularity. Perhaps because Chaplin's screen persona had always been calculated to be lovably disreputable—or perhaps simply because he was a man—the slurs did not finish him; his little tramp character would eventually do that unaided, a piece of self-inflicted type-casting that would lock him into his own past without offering him a future.

If mature men with a taste for young girls were a long-term fixture in Hollywood, the popularity of the Dickensian waif on-screen was slowly starting to decline by the 1930s. Only one actress had miraculously spanned the entire life of the phenomenon, sustaining a little girl image that began under the guidance of D. W. Griffith in 1909 and served her well for the next twenty years. She was Gladys Marie Smith from Toronto, Canada, reinvented as Little Mary Pickford for the American movies, a highly durable nymphet who, professionally at least, would have laughed at Humbert's age boundaries of nine and fourteen. Pickford was already seventeen when she appeared in Griffith's *The Heart of an Outlaw* (1909). A highly successful career based exclusively on playing little girls followed. This was typecasting of the most inflexible kind. When her legions of loyal fans were asked by a movie magazine in 1925 whom Little Mary should play next, Alice in Wonderland and Heidi were among the top choices. At the time Pickford was thirty-two, a studio boss (she was a 20 percent stakeholder in United Artists, sharing ownership with Charlie Chaplin, Douglas Fairbanks, and D. W. Griffith), and had been married to swashbuckling Fairbanks for five years.

In her long acting career she had brought her coy, ringleted presence to virtually every cinematized children's classic from *Pollyanna* to *Rebecca of Sunnybrook Farm*, as well as playing doll-clutching Gwendolyn in *The Poor Little Rich Girl* (1917) and Sara Crewe in *The Little Princess*. Her protracted adult depiction of a childhood that she had never personally experienced now looks rather grotesque, and her performances come over as skillful but cloying and arch. To her credit, Pickford did not think much of them herself ("I can't stand that sticky stuff"), and by the start of the 1930s she knew it was all over. Her fans would simply not let her grow up. When she had the temerity to bob her hair in 1929 they had been outraged. "You would have thought I had murdered someone," Pickford reminisced years later, "and in a sense I had."

— — —

By the 1930s Dickensian waifs were on their way out. Adults impersonating children were also passé, but children impersonating adults were becoming very popular indeed. In *This Is the Life* (1935), nine-year-old Jane Withers mimicked Marlene Dietrich's knowing top-hat-and-tails routine from *Blonde Venus* with disturbing skill. From *Mickey's Touchdown* (1933), a surviving still shows thirteen-year-old Mickey Rooney and seven-year-old Shirley Jean Rickert impersonating John Barrymore and Greta Garbo in an attitude of what looks like bored precoital languor at the foot of a staircase possibly belonging to a Grand Hotel (the title of a major movie hit from the year before).

One scene in the movie *Gold Diggers of 1933* features a midget, Billy Barty, disguised as a child of indeterminate sex, lasciviously raising a translucent curtain that has previously been displaying only the shapely silhouettes of scantily clad showgirls. (This tableau prefigures a rather more elegant one in the 1997 film of *Lolita* where sunlit sheets drying on a clothesline show Humbert only the teasing silhouette of his prepubescent quarry in the Haze garden.) Barty also appears in the 1933 movie *Footlight Parade*, once again grotesquely garbed in a baby bonnet, this time discovered hiding in their honeymoon bed by a newlywed couple (Dick Powell and Ruby Keeler). Thrown out of the room, the "child" becomes a voyeur at the keyhole. (Humbert, readers may recall, after an early mental breakdown ridicules a psychiatrist famous for making patients believe they had witnessed their own conception.)

These arch films, variants of a tradition that included Hal Roach's *Our Gang* series and the *Baby Burlesk* one-reelers, now look unsettling in a way that other film fantasies of the time do not. The camp charm of a movie like *42nd Street* (1933) is still enjoyable today, but our indulgent smile fades when the young "Chubby" Chaney passionately kisses a cardboard cutout of Greta Garbo stationed in a movie theater lobby in a 1931 *Our Gang* two-reeler.

The undisputed queen of the child-star adult impersonators was Miss Curly Top herself, Shirley Temple. Dauntingly precocious, the singing, dancing, acting Temple had emerged just as Pickford faded into the sunset, so firing the dreams of a thousand stage moms hoping to cash in on their own moppets. Hedda Hopper described the rush of Temple wannabes and their mothers as resembling "a flock of hungry locusts" descending on Tinseltown. Nathanael West would soon write a novel using the same image (*The Day of the Locust*, 1939) about Hollywood's losers and hopefuls that included a rather pathetic eight-year-old boy, Adore, and his steely stage mom ("What's Shirley Temple got that he ain't got?"). This novel preceded Eudora Welty's considerably less sympathetic portrait of an aggressively loud and clearly untalented tap-dancing child she dubs Shirley T. in her short story "Why I Live at the P.O." (1941).

It was Temple who set the standard, whether, at five years old, impersonating Marlene Dietrich (incredibly redubbed "Morelegs Sweettrick") in *Kid in Hollywood*, a 1933 *Baby Burlesk* short, or matching top adult dancers step for step as she became a seasoned trouper of eight years. Temple was not a nymphet, and neither were her contemporary child stars for that matter, but her precocity still posed an unsettling question about the sexual implications of the burlesque this particular baby was putting on. It was a matter that no one dared to raise in public until 1937.

Graham Greene's infamous review of the 1937 Shirley Temple movie *Wee Willie Winkie* in the urbane but obscure British magazine

Night and Day cast an intentional slur on a star Hollywood promoted as the embodiment of innocent cuteness. It may have been cute, but as far as Greene was concerned, it was hardly innocent. He wrote that nine-year-old Temple displayed "a certain adroit coquetry which appealed to middle-aged men." There was more.

> In *Captain January* she wore trousers with the mature suggestiveness of a Dietrich: her neat and well-developed rump twisted in the tap-dance: her naked eyes had a sidelong searching coquetry. Now in *Wee Willie Winkie*, wearing short kilts, she is completely totsy. . . . Watch the way she measures a man with agile studio eyes, with dimpled depravity [using] her well-shaped and desirable little body.

A swift libel suit by Twentieth Century Fox was successful and subsequently bankrupted the magazine, although it did little lasting harm to Greene, who swiftly decamped to Mexico, wrote *The Power and the Glory*, and, nearly twenty years later, became the first literary champion of a sensational American novel featuring a middle-aged man with a fatal taste for nymphets.

Greene's trenchant observations about Temple's sexualization were well founded but perhaps poorly targeted. *Wee Willie Winkie* was, after all, only one in a flood of similar films that adhered to a familiar convention, and it was perhaps selected for Greene's critical attention simply because it was directed by John Ford, already regarded as a serious director. On the other hand, Greene already seemed familiar with Temple in *Captain January*, which boasted a less exalted directorial hand.

The child-star movies of the thirties can be partially excused because they were part of a general climate in which the sexual tensions between middle-aged men and much younger women or girls were broadly accepted as moral-free dramatic conventions of the time. The arch fun of the infant-star vehicles was calculated to make them look innocent, and anyway more overtly sexual plots rarely risked provoking outrage by featuring actual children. As in the Swanson/Pickford days of twenty-something little girls, adults were recruited.

The Major and the Minor (1942) was something of a wild card for the period, revisiting the silent cinema's adult-imitating-a-child convention but this time seen through the caustic eye of Billy Wilder. Wilder was an Austrian expatriate who in many ways shared Stroheim's dark perspective but usually managed to channel it into very funny if sometimes cruel satire. *The Major and the Minor* revolves around midwestern innocent Susan Applegate (Ginger Rogers), who needs to get home to Iowa from New York but cannot afford the train fare. Disguising herself as a twelve-year-old in order to travel half price, she becomes involved with a shortsighted military man (Ray Milland) who finds himself strangely drawn to her. She feels the same, and the playing out of this apparently illicit romance lets Wilder have it both ways. The movie remains a very funny, out-of-time curio.

Otherwise, by the 1940s, the child-star syndrome had itself started to give way to a new type—adolescent girls who were sweet but not provocative, resourceful but not rebellious. They were not always the same actresses who had been cute tots, a hard lesson for some to learn. Temple was the first to discover her babyish talent might not be automatically parlayed into puberty and beyond. She never really made it past twelve and was finished by the time she was a teenager. Elizabeth Taylor, Judy Garland, and Deanna Durbin personified the older girl-child stereotype, more demure but certainly not without an appeal to middle-aged men. Taylor in the good-natured *Life with Father* is clearly a daddy's girl; *100 Men and a Girl*, despite its title, was an innocent "let's do the show right here" movie featuring a sweetly desirable Deanna Durbin and her incisive soprano voice; Garland, meanwhile, brought a no-nonsense, clean-pinafore charm to many films spanning the thirties and forties. She might have been the least sexy of that particular trio, but it was fourteen-year-old Garland upon whom MGM decided to bestow a crush for their thirty-five-year-old leading man Clark Gable. At Gable's birthday party, the studio got Garland to serenade him with "You Made Me Love You," and they then decided to commit the serenade to celluloid in *Broadway Melody of 1938*, where Garland duly sang the same song to a framed photograph of Gable.

Adolescent Garland and Durbin worked through the 1940s, winning over daddies and other crusty old men as and when the plot demanded. Despite their contrasting styles, both suffered from the same almost palpable demand from the studios and the public that they should simply never grow up. Garland's blossoming figure was strapped down and she was given diet pills, so starting her out on a lifetime of drug dependency that would end in despair and death at forty-seven. Durbin tried to make the transition to adult actress without success, despite her considerable beauty, and her career did not last beyond the 1940s; she went on to enjoy a long life away from Hollywood. Only Taylor made the breakthrough to an adult career, leaving behind a veritable menagerie of costars— dogs, horses, cats—as well as those men of a certain age. She had always looked older than her years, and her beauty when young was legendary. By the 1950s she would be costarring with young, handsome leading men: Montgomery Clift, James Dean, and Paul Newman. Taylor was the child star that got away, although in the end her career got away too, leaving her to bounce from unsuitable marriage to unsuitable marriage, an international headline grabber famous in the end for nothing but launching perfumes and being famous.

— — —

The nymphet was less conspicuously on view in the films of the 1940s, the decade that also marked the high point of film noir. With the sweeter adolescent girls taking over in the mainstream family entertainment movies, it was left to these shadowy crime movies to give house room to the occasional Lolita of the day, and those characters were usually one-offs—kid sisters or daughters whom circumstance and their own sex drive put on the horns of a moral dilemma that was usually not the main concern of the movie. If Lauren Bacall was the smokily erotic sensation of *The Big Sleep* (1946), it was Martha Vickers as her racy little sister who peddled the more provocative sex. "She tried to sit on my lap when I was standing up" is the deadpan response of private eye Philip Marlowe (Humphrey Bogart) to her first overture. In *Double Indemnity* (1944) it is amoral femme fatale Phyllis Dietrichson's adolescent stepdaughter Lola who seems undecided between going off the rails with a young hood or pulling herself together. And the most sensational 1940s child-molesting story was in the end provided not by Hollywood's product but by one of its more colorful performers.

Errol Leslie Thomson Flynn started life in Hobart, Tasmania, and was something of an adventurer before he arrived in Hollywood by way of the provincial British stage in 1935. The 1940s proved to be Errol Flynn's golden decade, and he appeared in a series of swashbuckling period movies that included *The Adventures of Robin Hood* and *The Adventures of Don Juan* while living the life of the Hollywood playboy to the hilt. Good-looking and with a rakish good humor, he enjoyed enormous success—indeed, it would be hard to find anyone who enjoyed it more. His taste for underage girls was well known around town and eventually well known in the world's tabloids. Two teenagers, Peggy Satterlee and Betty Hansen, accused him of statutory rape in 1942, but Flynn was eventually acquitted after a twenty-one-day trial. Wives came and went, but Flynn's taste for young girls would continue unchallenged until the end of the 1940s, when he was again involved in a statutory rape case, this time of a fifteen-year-old girl. Again he was acquitted. Flynn never sought to disguise his tastes, and one of the things that had counted against him in the 1942 rape case had been Peggy Satterlee's evidence that he called her "J.B." ("jail bait") and "S.Q.Q." ("San Quentin quail")—proof, it was submitted, that he knew she was a juvenile. That time he got off because his accusers were eventually shown to be less than inexperienced before they met Flynn, further evidence that men could expect to get away with more than women in such matters.

It seemed the movies' preoccupation with children and light family comedies was beginning to wane at the end of the 1940s. It may have been due to nothing more than overexposure, or it may have been that the sobering experience of World War II—even if that experience was only tasted by some through the movie theater newsreels—had encouraged a taste for grittier fare than recycled Victorian dimples and ringlets. Gloria Grahame, Veronica Lake, and Lauren Bacall may not have been much older than Elizabeth Taylor, but the shadowy, crime-ridden milieus they inhabited on-screen represented adult entertainment that seemed more in keeping with the times. Then again, it may have been nothing more than that the postwar baby boom starting to populate America's homes with large numbers of real children made movies starring unreal children seem suddenly less appealing. The last working representative of the 1940s child star turned adolescent songstress was Gloria Jean Schoonover who, as Gloria Jean, gamely tried to take on Deanna Durbin's mantle (she was five years younger) as every moviegoer's sweetheart. Gloria Jean had costarred with Bing Crosby in *If I Had My Way* (1940) and then went on to make twenty more largely forgettable films for Universal over the next ten years. Like Lolita she had been robbed of her childhood by an adult agenda initially represented by thirty-eight-year-old producer

Joe Pasternak. Marooned in a fairytale world of studio-funded special tutors and voice coaches, and rubbing shoulders with some of the biggest stars of the day, Gloria Jean gave her all to a style of sweet adolescent musical film fantasy that was in terminal decline but the production of which still represented the only reality she had ever known. She might have gotten a reality check from the star of the one bracing film she did appear in—*Never Give a Sucker an Even Break* (1941), where she played the niece of morose child hater W. C. Fields—but Gloria Jean had started too late, and when the end came it came abruptly. She moved into television and then into obscurity. Soon she was earning a living as a receptionist. The sweet-voiced little movie princesses had not made it into the next decade, and Gloria Jean had been the last one to leave, and it fell to her to turn out the light. The 1950s would be the province of a new breed of adult women displaying childlike qualities—pneumatic Marilyn Monroe and Jayne Mansfield, ambivalent Carroll Baker and Judy Holliday, waiflike Audrey Hepburn and Leslie Caron. In the background, still just a literary phenomenon, Lolita was waiting to make her sensational first impact on American popular culture, unmistakeably symbolizing a new melding of childlike innocence and adult sexuality.

[5]

LOLITA IN MOVIELAND 2:
"Pedophilia Is a Hard Sell" ╱

MARILYN MONROE HAD BEEN PLAYING BIT PARTS IN MOVIES SINCE 1947. She had been a girl working in a juke joint in the juvenile delinquent movie *Dangerous Years*; she was little more than an extra in the 1920s-set musical *You Were Meant for Me*; she played the anonymous "Girl in Canoe" in the corny outdoors comedy *Scudda Hoo! Scudda Hay!*; and she was the prettiest of the hookers pretending to be showgirls in the lightweight Western *Ticket to Tomahawk* (1950). Also in 1950, however, she made the transition to more substantial movies with a memorable appearance as Louis Calhern's mistress in John Huston's *The Asphalt Jungle*. From there it looked as if Monroe might progress toward a serious, if limited, acting career. Instead, about half of the twenty-two films she appeared in during the 1950s helped to define her as the ultimate Hollywood sex goddess and one whose erotic charge was indivisible from what would become one of the decade's chief preoccupations: childish feminine innocence wrapped up in an adult body. Monroe's body was not just adult; it was almost a caricature of a fully formed woman; ample breasts, curvy hips, bleached hair, and lots of lipstick were the visible assets. But they were paired with a wide-eyed expression and a mannered, breathy little voice that signaled childish ingenuousness.

"Why don't you ever get a dress like that?" says the midwestern businessman to his wife as Monroe sashays past in a shimmering fuchsia number in an early scene from *Niagara* (1953). "Listen," his spouse replies dryly, "for a dress like that, you've got to start laying plans when you're about thirteen." The droll phrase "laying plans" suggested a scheming streak to be found in certain girls precociously aware of the sexual power to be gained from cultivating a provocative appearance early on. Did Lolita, at "about thirteen," start laying plans to become a world-famous teenage sex symbol? Did Monroe? In *Niagara* she is a humorless vamp, but soon, especially in comedies, she would cultivate a playful manner of breathy innocence as a counterbalance to her appearance. As Clive James once noted, European movie sirens like Greta Garbo and Sophia Loren might look as if they were unashamedly thinking about sex, but "Monroe looked as if [sex] was something that might easily happen to her while she was thinking about something else."

In the Howard Hawks comedy *Monkey Business* (1952), a youth elixir causes pretty much the whole cast to regress into childish behavior at some point or other, and much of the fun comes from seeing Ginger Rogers, Cary Grant, Charles Coburn, and Marilyn Monroe rise to the challenge of enacting infantilism—except that for Monroe it is really not that much of a stretch. Ginger Rogers is terrific at metamorphosing into a kid, but a childish Monroe does not behave all that differently from the adult model that she was already refining in 1952 and that would soon become iconic. At one point Dr. Barnaby Fulton (Grant) defends the behavior of Monroe's character Lois Laurel by saying, "She's half child." His wife (Rogers) replies dryly, "Not the half that shows."

The half that showed was slavishly copied by Jayne Mansfield, Mamie van Doren, and other less successful 1950s bottle blondes. They were less successful because they did not have the other half, the inner child. Monroe had the 1950s version of the damaged little Victorian girl syndrome and projected it with an impersonation of mental vacuity, physical vulnerability, and a constant need for a father figure to look after her. Because hers was an image based on reality, Monroe was the one who caught the public's imagination; in real life she was a little brighter than she pretended to be on-screen and she could throw off the perilously high heels when she got home, but the deep-seated need for a daddy was genuine and would be evidenced by the men she sought and occasionally married.

Interestingly, a far more subtly shaded version of the Monroe image had been enshrined in Judy Holliday's most famous performance, that of Billie Dawn, originally created for Garson Kanin's smart Broadway play *Born Yesterday* but subsequently repeated in the 1950 film version too. Uneducated, streetwise, and feisty, Billie cuts a potentially tragic figure as she outgrows her ex-showgirl personality as the bored mistress of a boorish self-made millionaire. One day she will be replaced with a younger model, but until then she cheerfully admits to playing dumb to get what she wants, only gradually realizing that being sugar daddy's little girl is not enough—this Lolita will have to learn to talk for herself and put her mind to good use. Her demonstration of a dormant intelligence gradually reawakened and then vigorously expressed is both hilarious and touching. Holliday, who was to die young, reprised variants of Billie Dawn in a handful of less satisfactory films, but her signature performance as a not-so-dumb blonde still stands as a classic example of how to make a cliché live and breathe.

— — —

Audrey Hepburn could not have made a greater physical contrast with the curvy dumb blonde type, being stick thin and brunette, but she too succeeded with a 1950s image that frequently seemed to hover between childhood and womanhood. In *Roman Holiday* (1953), she is an adult princess solemnly constrained by royal protocol until she escapes to have distinctly girlish fun in the Italian capital with Gregory Peck's expatriate journalist who is at first unaware of her identity. The entire plot of Billy Wilder's *Sabrina* (1954) revolves around Hepburn's ambivalence as the tellingly named Sabrina Fairchild. Her character's transformation from the Long Island chauffeur's little girl who is ignored by her dream male, society playboy Robert Larrabee (William Holden), into a sophisticated young woman who returns from a two-year stint in Paris to captivate him simply dramatizes the innate duality of her appeal. Larrabee does not even recognize the revamped Sabrina as the little girl he has vaguely known all her life, although to the audience she looks much the same, except for the classier wardrobe.

In *Love in the Afternoon* (1957), adapted from a French novel, fifty-six-year-old Gary Cooper's Frank Flannagan has an affair with twenty-eight-year-old Hepburn's Ariane Chavasse. The May/December plot is the point, but Cooper was just four years away from death and Hepburn still looks younger than her years, making this one of Billy Wilder's more dispiriting films, although one much in keeping with the fashion of the day.

Otto Preminger's lackluster movie of another French novel, *Bonjour Tristesse*, was watchable only for Jean Seberg's believable portrayal of a teenager with an unhealthy fixation on her playboy father. The book and its themes are discussed later, but this poor film really only paid lip service to its source—and reinforced the growing sense that as the 1950s progressed the young were being given an ever greater license to be sexual beings in their own right.

Outside of cinema the trend was more noticeable; the young were grabbing the initiative without even applying for a license. Rock 'n' roll had arrived, and its new male stars, led by Elvis Presley, sold raw sex wrapped up in a new music that alienated parents, excited their sons, and aroused their daughters. A few movies tentatively tried to absorb rock 'n' roll, but apart from the diverting *The Girl Can't Help It* (1956) they were almost without exception embarrassing demonstrations that mainstream movies and rebellious rock were worlds apart. Meanwhile, *Lolita*'s publication was cutting across cultural boundaries and putting underage sex into headlines that were read by millions who would never read Nabokov's book. Lolita would have to wait until the next decade for her first screen appearance, but before that happened a much more explosive package was provided by the combined talents of Tennessee Williams, Elia Kazan, and Carroll Baker.

The child bride sleeps. Virginal Baby Doll Meighan (Carroll Baker) lies on a crib while her Peeping Tom husband ogles her through a hole in the wall. (*Baby Doll*, 1956, Warner Bros.)

The notorious *Baby Doll*, Williams's screen adaptation of his
own lusty and comic one-act play *Twenty-Seven Wagons Full of Cotton*, was a visually striking black-and-white film revolving around
the childlike nineteen-year-old bride of failed Mississippi cotton
gin owner Archie Lee Meighan (Karl Malden). As the result of
what sounds like a peculiarly Mississippian prenuptial agreement,
Baby Doll Meighan is withholding sex from her husband until
her twentieth birthday—although she seems rather less inhibited
when it comes to Archie's dynamic business rival Silva (Eli Wal-
lach). The exceptionally beautiful young Carroll Baker played Baby
Doll earthily enough to outrage the Catholic Legion of Decency
and prompt *Time* magazine to call this the "dirtiest American-
made motion picture ever . . . legally exhibited." The film's notoriety (emblemized by an iconic still showing Baby Doll wearing
the short nightgown that would henceforth carry her name, sucking her thumb, and sleeping on a child's crib with the slats down)
was enough to prompt fainthearted Warner Bros. into withdrawing the film from national release during its pre-Christmas 1956
run. Half a century after the furor it caused, *Baby Doll* looks better
than ever, an edgy mix of comedy and drama, adult sexual promise and adolescent teasing, shadows and sunlight, tragedy and
farce, all presented in ravishing black-and-white cinematography.
Utterly at odds with all other prevailing characteristics of 1950s
films, *Baby Doll* actually went straight to the heart of the decade's
premier sexual preoccupation: that special appeal of the child in
a woman's body. In an interesting footnote, when Pennsylvanian
Carroll Baker made the trip to Mississippi to star in the film, she
found that "baby doll" was a universal form of address for young
women there, a sobriquet that seemed to combine the familiar
"baby" with a built-in reminder of women's essentially passive,
not to say submissive, role. White rock 'n' roll, being born nearby
(Presley, of course, came from Tupelo, Mississippi, and lived just

across the border in Memphis for most of his adult life), was quick
to incorporate "baby" into its vernacular, and the very first rocker
to write his own number one hit was Texan Buddy Knox with the
song "Party Doll."

Most mainstream fifties movies continued to pussyfoot around
the latest child/woman stereotype, and the rather grubby Oscar-
winning Lerner and Loewe musical *Gigi* (1958) was no exception.
Based on a 1945 novel by Sidonie-Gabrielle Colette, its high-society
plot revolves around the grooming of a prostitute played by the
elfin Leslie Caron, who at twenty-seven could easily pass for the
adolescent she was supposed to be. One can only wonder where
the Catholic Legion of Decency and all the other right-wing moral
guardians were when, in CinemaScope and with a G rating, Maurice Chevalier, a musical Humbert if ever there was one, celebrated
the unripe appeal of Caron's pubescent whore-in-training with his
lasciviously delivered song "Thank Heaven for Little Girls."

The year 1956 saw the release of another iconoclastic movie
about childhood, Mervyn LeRoy's film of *The Bad Seed*, based
on Maxwell Anderson's play of the same name. A compelling if
badly flawed movie, it focuses on eight-year-old Rhoda (played by
eleven-year-old Patty McCormack) who appears to be a stereotyp-
ical little miss Goody Two-Shoes complete with dirndl and blonde
braids, but who is eventually revealed as a killer. Her doting dad
is mainly absent, her mother seems beguiled by her, and only a
simpleminded handyman divines her chilling capacity for evil.
Utterly at odds with the family entertainment mood of the decade,
the film only seems to lose its nerve at the end when it executes
its pint-sized killer with a ludicrous thunderbolt sent from heaven
via the script department and then undercuts its own conclusion
with an absurd theatrical curtain call where the entire cast troops
through the living room, and Rhoda's mother playfully punishes
her as if for some minor domestic mischief. Most reviews of the

time admired its nerve while deploring its decline into uneasy farce in the second half. Even so, *The Bad Seed* marks a groundbreaking Hollywood depiction of the darker side of a female child who uses her stereotypically cute looks and presumed innocence to deceive. Shirley Temple, after all, would never have played a pint-sized ax murderer.

Nubile Nancy Bowden (Lori Martin) cowers as convicted rapist Max Cady stalks her in the 1962 original version of *Cape Fear*. (*Cape Fear*, 1962, Universal)

Made in the same year as the first movie version of *Lolita*, the original film version of *Cape Fear*, directed by J. Lee Thompson, featured Robert Mitchum as Max Cady, a vindictive ex-prisoner intent upon exacting revenge from the lawyer who helped to put him away for attacking a woman eight and a half years before. It contained particularly graphic scenes of Cady attacking both his enemy's wife and young daughter. British director Thompson had already made many workmanlike (and one or two excellent) films—his output included *Tiger Bay*, *The Guns of Navarone*, and *Mackenna's Gold*—but he was a lifelong opponent of censorship and battled spiritedly with the American censor who sought to reduce the general violence and tone down Cady's obvious intention to rape the lawyer's teenage daughter. Thompson had originally wanted sixteen-year-old Hayley Mills to play the daughter ("because she was a very sexual girl"), but ironically enough the very sexual girl was under contract to Disney. Thompson wound up with the rather more anodyne Lori Martin instead. Although far less forthright than Martin Scorsese's 1991 version of the story (where the daughter actually appears to be aroused by stalker Cady and at one point shares an open-mouth kiss with him), Thompson's film, aided by a superb Bernard Herrmann score, manages to suggest extreme menace where it cannot be explicit. When Cady finally corners and assaults the lawyer's wife on a houseboat, he tries to get her to trade her own rape for sparing her daughter in a scene that is full of darkly suggestive detail. At one point Cady snatches up an egg from a counter and violently crushes it in his fist, spraying yolk and white on his victim's chest and shoulders and then smearing the mess with the palm of his hand. Not for the first time a determined director discovered that when the censor obliged oblique methods instead of obvious ones, the result could be just as disturbing.

Censorship was to become ever more toothless as the 1960s progressed, and by 1968 the laissez-faire mood assisted by the hippie culture meant Hollywood felt relaxed enough to release Christian Marquand's supremely vulgar and jokily pedophilic *Candy*, a film version of Terry Southern's erotic novel that was itself loosely based on Voltaire's *Candide*. In *Candy*, a high school girl's naivete accompanies her on a sexual odyssey involving one dirty old man after another, each some sort of pillar of society. James Coburn, Walter Matthau, John Huston, Charles Aznavour, Richard Burton, and Marlon Brando all play various lecherous contemporary father figures (while, interestingly, Florinda Bolkan plays a minor character called Lolita). Most critics properly dubbed the film a dreadful mess, but this was the heyday of the swinging sixties and hardly any of them seemed troubled by its blatant child exploitation overtones.

Everybody would be troubled by the one biggest—and certainly the longest-running—sex-with-a-minor Hollywood story to dominate the headlines since the passing of Errol Flynn. Started in 1977, it centered on film director Roman Polanski, and its reverberations still continue to be felt over thirty years later. If Flynn had been a colorful old-school fortune hunter left over from the days of empire, Roman Polanski (Rajmund Roman Liebling) was a more troubled child of World War II, born in Paris in 1933 to a Jewish father and Catholic mother. In a piece of fatal bad timing, the family returned to Poland just before the Nazis invaded; his mother was to die in Auschwitz, his father barely survived another concentration camp, and the young Roman only just escaped the Jewish ghetto. With such a traumatic start to his life, the various tragedies that he was to encounter later are put into a salutary perspective. Even so, when, in 1969, his pregnant wife Sharon Tate was murdered in the most grotesque and sensational circumstances at their house in the Hollywood Hills, Polanski—who had been absent at the time—was totally devastated and entered a phase that saw him shuttling between the United States and Europe until, in 1977, he met the thirteen-year-old Samantha Geimer. In retrospect, Polanski, like Chaplin, could later be seen to have included many clues about his sexual preferences in the eight movies he had made after leaving Poland. *Cul-de-Sac* (1966) cast Françoise Dorleac as a spoiled little girl in an adult woman's body, forever taunting her emasculated husband but finally taken in hand and beaten with a belt by the gangster who bursts into their remote island home. The broadly comic *Dance of the Vampires* had Sharon Tate as Sarah Shagal (!), the nubile innkeeper's daughter whose father spanks her as one of the guests plays Peeping Tom through a stylized key-hole. Perhaps the most revealing of Polanski's Freudian movies is, however, one of the least known. Variously titled *What?* and (in a censored U.S. version) *Diary of Forbidden Dreams*, this 1972 film is nothing less than a loose erotic reworking of *Alice's Adventures in Wonderland*, in which young American tourist Nancy (Sydne Rome) has some very strange adventures of her own in an Italian coastal town. A disjointed film even before the censor got at it, *What?* transforms Alice's rabbit hole into a strange villa peopled with nightmarish inhabitants, one of whom is a retired pimp played by Marcello Mastroianni. A scene in which he interrogates Nancy with all the logic of the Black Queen and then shackles her wrists to her ankles and whips her with a switch is the main reason this film never received a mainstream theatrical release and is still little seen; the handling of the scene is kinky and jokey, and its presence offers further evidence that Polanski's sexual ideal was a young girl upon whom male dominance could be played out in ritualistic sex games.

Even Polanski's late-blooming film noir masterpiece, *Chinatown* (1974), turns on the childhood sexual trauma of Faye Dunaway's character, Evelyn Mulwray. Once raped by her father (John Huston), she continues to protect the identity of a mysterious young girl called Katherine until, in response to a series of face slaps from Jack Nicholson's exasperated private eye, she finally answers alternately, "My sister. My daughter. My sister. My daughter . . . she's my sister and my daughter." Unlike many of Polanski's earlier films, *Chinatown* is no black comedy but an elegant and haunting tragedy, yet it too features a powerful and abusive old man whose control of politicians and policemen is echoed in his iron rule of his family. The implication of the film's somber ending is that he now wants to gain control of Katherine, his daughter/granddaughter, in order to repeat the abuse—echoes of Humbert's idle musings that had he and Lolita crossed the Mexican border instead of returning east to Beardsley, he might, in time, have impregnated her and had her produce a Lolita the Second who would be eight or nine when he was still in the prime of his life.

Polanski's films benefited from the dark strand of sex that ran through most of them, but his real-life fondness for submissive young girls was to stir up all kinds of trouble. When Samantha Geimer caught Polanski's eye, he immediately asked her mother if he could photograph her for the French edition of *Vogue*. Consent was given and a private shoot arranged. Geimer claimed to have felt uncomfortable during the shoot, especially when Polanski asked her to undress in front of him. Even so, she agreed to a second shoot at a house, allegedly on Jack Nicholson's estate in Los Angeles's Mulholland district. There she alleged that Polanski gave her a cocktail of champagne and quaaludes prior to raping and sodomizing her. Polanski was arrested in the lobby of the Beverly Wilshire hotel, where he was staying at the time, and subsequently charged. After a plea bargain the drugs and perversion charges were reduced to one of engaging in unlawful sexual intercourse with a minor. Polanski's version was that Geimer's mother had effectively entrapped him with a view to blackmail. Fearing that the plea bargain would not be honored, Polanski left the United States before trial, never to return. He is a French citizen, and France has no extradition agreement with the United States. He remains a European director who has never since set foot in the United States or any country that has extradition agreements with the United States.

– – –

Preteen prostitution featured in Martin Scorsese's *Taxi Driver* (1976), with Jodie Foster causing a minor stir with her portrayal of twelve-year-old whore Iris Steensma. Foster herself had started performing at the age of three, displaying her bare buttocks in ads for Coppertone, a brand whose shtick was to accentuate a golden tan by contrasting it with the white marks left by removed bikini bottoms. Iris comes into the psychopathic saga of Travis Bickle quite late, but she provides him with a crucial catalyst for launching his murderous assault on her pimp and his associates. Oblivious to her claims that her life isn't so bad, Bickle forces her into the symbolic role of Innocence Defiled, which allows him to unleash his volcano of violence against The City that has been building up throughout the movie.

Also in 1976, heavily disguised as a Hitchcockian thriller, came the ultimate daddy's little girl movie, Brian de Palma's *Obsession*. Paul Schrader's tour de force script has a successful New Orleans businessman lose his wife and young daughter in a kidnapping when he refuses to pay the ransom and a police rescue attempt goes fatally wrong. Ten years later, he meets a girl in Italy who looks exactly like his dead wife. He becomes obsessed with her, they have an affair, and he makes plans to take her back to New Orleans and marry her. Eventually the whole Italian episode is revealed to be an elaborate revenge plan: the born-again wife is actually the daughter who, unknown to everyone, survived the kidnapping and is now intent on exacting revenge from her neglectful daddy. In a Freudian nightmare of a scene, the daughter/lover, played by Geneviève Bujold, is shown toggling between her two roles (high camera angle/low camera angle, little girl's voice/woman's voice) during the course of a single breathless walk along an airport corridor. In Schrader's original script incest took place, but by the time the film was shot and edited, de Palma decided to fudge the issue.

Two years later, Louis Malle's *Pretty Baby* would ruffle rather more feathers with its unsweetened story of Violet (thirteen-year-old Brooke Shields), the eponymous pretty baby raised in a turn-

of-the-century New Orleans brothel where her virginity is pragmatically auctioned by her mother. We are down South again in the
land of baby, and this baby clings to her doll, just like Lilian Gish
used to, but not to aid an impersonation of extreme youth—Brooke
Shields *was* extremely young. As Violet she appears naked several
times and at one point is severely beaten for making mischievous
sexual advances to a young black boy. When she runs away from
the brothel and illegally marries a photographer (who takes a formal picture of her as a reclining nude), his pre-wedding gift to her
is a doll "because every child should have a doll." It seems safe to
assume that such a movie might not be made today. The photographer, Ernest J. Bellocq (played by Keith Carradine), evokes shades
of Charles L. Dodgson and his photographic studies of little girls
previously discussed.

In 1978, Louis Malle directed *Pretty Baby*, an ambivalent soft-
focus movie in which thirteen-year-old Brooke Shields went topless
as child prostitute Violet in early twentieth-century New Orleans.
(*Pretty Baby*, 1978, Paramount)

In the late 1970s, Woody Allen was in the middle of one of his most productive periods of moviemaking. Critics sometimes argued that he kept making the same movie over and over again, a variable celebration of loves found and loves lost from the same neurotic New York perspective of an intellectual with doubts about everything, especially mothers, psychoanalysis, and Judaism. Even for the most skeptical critics however, *Manhattan* (1979) represented one of Allen's most satisfying variants on the theme. With its sumptuous black-and-white photography, Allen's love affair with New York City featured the usual character list of literati and well-heeled academics but this time introduced a new element, a seventeen-year-old girlfriend for Allen's midforties character. This age discrepancy is a central concern of the movie, never better highlighted than in the scene where Allen, Diane Keaton, and Michael Murphy are walking down the street having a very pretentious discussion about art while the seventeen-year-old girlfriend, Tracy (Mariel Hemingway), tags along. "What do you do, Tracy?" asks Keaton's character suddenly, in the middle of talking about the latest profile she has been commissioned to write for an arts magazine.

"I go to high school," Tracy replies innocently.

Suppressing a smile, Keaton turns aside to Murphy and says in a barely audible undertone, "Somewhere Nabokov is smiling, if you know what I mean."

No one was smiling when, thirteen years later, Allen's relationship with his girlfriend's adopted daughter was revealed. Now the age difference was thirty-five years, and the good-natured, liberal *Manhattan* was suddenly looked at in a new light by a moralizing press and public. It remains, however, one of the few examples of an American movie—a comedy to boot—that takes an adult, bittersweet approach to such relationships. Although *Manhattan* is most commonly referred to as Allen's love letter to New York City, it is also Allen's love letter to young women, and Mariel

Hemingway supplied a miraculously touching performance as a Lolita who was not only allowed to express her own point of view but one who emerged from the affair looking graceful, generous, and optimistic.

In *Pretty Baby* there is more than a hint of Lewis Carroll about Keith Carradine's Bellocq, seen here photographing his child bride (Brooke Shields), for whom he has just bought a doll. (*Pretty Baby*, 1978, Paramount)

– – –

Adrian Lyne's 1997 attempt to cinematize *Lolita* is discussed in detail later, but in the present context it is worth noting that the thoughtful adaptation written by Stephen Schiff was greeted by a reactionary response that shrieked disapproval long before the film was completed or, in some cases, even begun. It was symptomatic of a new unwillingness to address stories focusing on pedophilia that would persist into the next millennium. The news media's increasingly emotive and sensationalist treatment of child abuse cases in the 1990s had helped to create a popular mood of national outrage at not only any actual instances of pedophilia but also at any film, TV program, play, or book that dared to explore the topic. This sense of outrage was a knee-jerk reaction unmodified by rational thought, but the public mood was unmistakable. The resulting film "censorship" was less a case of official proscription, more an informal outcome of a mixture of moral cowardice and commercial timidity shown by movie producers and studio executives who feared that acknowledging child abuse in a movie would automatically result in catastrophic box office returns.

Then in 2004 came Nicole Kassell's groundbreaking film of Steven Fechter's play *The Woodsman.* An honorable bid to explore a variety of issues raised by a pedophile newly released from prison who is uncertainly seeking reform or redemption but fears recidivism, this R-rated movie was never destined for box office success. But it did mark one of American cinema's most painfully honest attempts to deal with the subject. Kevin Bacon's fine performance as child molester Walter is complemented by an extraordinary cameo from Hannah Pilkes. She plays Robin, the eleven-year-old girl Walter ominously befriends toward the end of the film and who, politely turning down his offer to let her sit on his lap as they talk on a park bench, goes on to hint at her experience of molestation at home. She says little but her omissions are eloquent, and her sudden quiet tears confirm a deep sadness devoid of anger. What if, you wonder, Humbert's bravura assurances that twelve-year-old Lolita was unaware of what she was doing on his lap was just another outrageous piece of misdirection?

A postmodern movie take on the Lolita syndrome was always in the cards but did not appear until some sixty years after moviegoing Lo, Hummy, and Mummy absorbed a diet of simple morality tales variously set in the Old West, the new asphalt jungle, or the timeless musical theater. *Hard Candy* (2005), directed by David

Slade and written by Brian Nelson, iconoclastically inverted the familiar story of an older man preying on an underage girl and set it in the age of the Web.

A vengeful Lolita for the twenty-first century. In *Hard Candy*, Ellen Page plays Hayley Stark (a.k.a. thonggrrrl14) who has no intention of becoming the fourteen-year-old victim of the thirty-two-year-old man who believes he is grooming her on the Internet. (*Hard Candy*, 2005, Vulcan)

"In *Hard Candy*, an Internet Lolita Is Not as Innocent as She Looks" ran the rather literal headline to Manohla Dargis's *New York Times* review of the film. It is something of an understatement. Garbed in a Little Red Riding Hood outfit that, for those who recall Nicolas Roeg's *Don't Look Now* (1973), may evoke memories of another very ambiguous little girl, this new Lolita for the cyberage also seems to be a spiritual cousin of Charles Bronson's character in the retributive *Death Wish* series.

Starting hypnotically with nothing more than a computer screen display, the film introduces its two principals, thirty-two-year-old photographer Jeff Kohlver (lensman319) and fourteen-year old Hayley Stark (thonggrrrl14), through their flirtatious text conversation on-screen. Although characterized by improbably rapid typing and faultless spelling, theirs is a mesmerizingly believable dialog that ends with an arrangement to meet in person for the first time. The tryst is at a cafe ominously called Nighthawks, taking its name and its logo from the famous Edward Hopper painting.

At Nighthawks, thonggrrrl14 turns out to be a very wholesome-looking young teen, the antithesis of the lurid Lolita stereotype and indeed, as embodied by Ellen Page, surely a ringer for Nabokov's Lolita, she of the chestnut hair and the juvenile breasts. Jeff (Patrick Wilson) also seems more personable in the flesh than he did in his slightly creepy lensman319 persona. The twist comes early, when Hayley encourages Jeff to take her back to his isolated bachelor pad where it is she who spikes his drink and then takes him prisoner before subjecting him to a regime of physical and psychological torture based on her conviction that he is a pedophile and a murderer. The assumed prey was the hunter from the start, and the protracted playing out of this newly reversed situation soon becomes rather muddled despite riveting performances from Page and Wilson. Still, *Hard Candy* is interesting for a number of peripheral reasons. Several reviews referenced Lolita ("What Hayley says and does to her Internet Humbert Humbert firmly makes the case that this avenging angel is really the demon daughter of Valerie Solanas and Lorena Bobbitt," wrote Manohla Dargis). Canadian actress Ellen Page's stunning metamorphosis from breathless young teen to self-assured psychopath in the space of a couple of hours surely draws a definitive line under those early movies in which youngsters were admired for successfully aping the manners and mannerisms of adults.

From the very first scene of the film the cultural references come thick and fast, but they mainly emanate from Hayley, not Jeff. On-screen he playfully calls her "baby." She keys back, "would a baby read zadie smith?" authentically disdainful of capital letters except for emphasis, as in "JOKE!" She takes a Donna Tartt novel to Night-hawks in case he stands her up. Later, this fourteen-year-old child of the twenty-first century says she is reading about minor American actress Jean Seberg (1938–1979). Seberg—the precocious teen lead in *Bonjour Tristesse*—also played the title character in Robert Rossen's *Lilith* (1964), an unhappily prescient story about a mentally disturbed young woman confined to an East Coast sanitarium. Seberg herself was a victim of chronic depression who made several suicide attempts before finally succeeding in the backseat of a car in a Paris suburb. Hayley sums up her life matter-of-factly, saying, "She slept with the wrong people and ended up killing herself." Hayley also claims to like the recherché British electronica duo Goldfrapp (whom she actually loathes) to see if Jeff will use the classic grooming ploy of pretending to like them too. She notes that whenever he failed to pick up on certain online allusions of hers there was a delay while he frantically looked up the source on the Internet before pretending to have gotten the reference all along ("You used all the same phrases to talk about Goldfrapp as they use in the reviews on amazon.com"). Here is a pleasing inversion of Humbert's aloof tendency to use arcane Eurocentric cultural references, a private lexical amusement arcade that is largely meaningless to Lolita but that identifies Humbert as a man of the world, in every sense. In *Hard Candy* it is the successful professional photographer—the character we might reasonably assume to be the man of the world—who is totally outmaneuvered by a dangerously precocious child for whom the subtleties, reference points, and moral logic of the Internet culture come as second nature. *Hard Candy*'s inspiration apparently came from Japanese news reports of girls ambushing men seeking underage dates on the Internet. Their tactic and *Hard Candy*'s reductio ad absurdum of it looks, in the end, less like female empowerment and more like the sort of warfare that brings both parties down into the mud, so rendering them indistinguishable from one another. Is Hayley really a Lolita for our time? Hardly. In truth, of all the ostensible neo-Lolitas in recent history's hall of distorting mirrors, Hayley may be among the least plausible. When Dolores Haze sentenced Humbert to death she did it not with a noose but by accident, through her complete indifference to his late-blooming love and by divulging Quilty's identity. The melancholic scene where she waves homicidal Dad good-bye one last time from the step of her sad Coalmont home can have only one outcome. Yet Lolita was only ever carelessly, thoughtlessly unkind, whereas thonggrrrl14 (and that snarling spelling, if nothing else in *Hard Candy*, would surely have been enjoyed by wordsmith Nabokov) is a self-appointed vigilante with a solemn cause, exactly the kind of political character Lolita's creator famously abhorred.

[6]

ON THE ROAD:
Lolita's Moving Prison

CRUCIAL TO ANY UNDERSTANDING OF NABOKOV'S NYMPHET IS ONE of the most exuberant parts of Nabokov's novel: the yearlong road trip. This eleven-and-a-half-thousand-word section comes at the middle of the book and marks the point of no return for Humbert. It also contains some of the novel's most revealing details about Lolita herself, details that frequently emerge not in the course of one of Humbert's typically solipsistic character assessments but very much in the margins of their twenty-seven-thousand-mile journey.

Having collected his now-motherless stepdaughter from Camp Q, her New England summer camp, in August 1947, Humbert commits himself and her to what is in effect an abduction à LaSalle, taking his newly conscripted twelve-year-old lover on a protracted, sprawling, fugitive tour of the United States. He believes that by traveling as vacationing father and daughter they will raise none of the suspicions that setting up home together in a community might provoke. On the move, Lolita will not be able to make regular friends (in whom she might confide and thus betray him), and there will be no schools, psychologists, or social workers. Instead there will just be a year in limbo, disguised as a vacation for a child who has recently lost her mother in tragic circumstances. What is good for Humbert—the opportunity to enjoy Lolita's body night after night with impunity—effectively robs her of twelve months of her childhood. It also insidiously turns her into a pet prostitute, as she discovers that the sex she is obliged to provide (under Humbert's threat of being turned over to reform school or juvenile detention home) is still in part a negotiable favor with its own tawdry sliding scale of rewards for different gratifications.

It is perhaps tempting to think of this tour—in however debased a form—as being in the general spirit of the Great American Road Trip, that iconic celebration of freedom, optimism, and exploration expressed by driving across a geographically varied nation. After all, Humbert, at least by his own lights, does have something to celebrate. It soon becomes clear, though, that this particular journey inverts most of the popular expectations of the classic road trip, imprisoning its participants rather than freeing them and denying them any destination other than a grudging and inevitable return to their starting point. Simultaneously, it feeds Humbert's paranoia about retributive authorities in the shape of an ever-shifting cast of prying policemen, probing motel proprietors, and worryingly inquisitive strangers. As Lolita's self-appointed jailer, Humbert is in his own way as much a prisoner of their odyssey as she is. Yet it is perhaps worth remembering that in searching for freedom or inspiration not all Great American Road Trippers have always been happily enchanted hunters.

Henry Miller's dyspeptic tour of 1940s America, *The Air-Conditioned Nightmare*, amounts to little more than a litany of complaints about capitalism, mass media, rapacious industry, easy credit, misinformation, and what Miller called "the divorce between man and nature." The haunting photographs comprising Robert Frank's 1959 book *The Americans* evoke a very unromantic voyage of discovery: a stone-faced young waitress beneath a "Merry Christmas" sign in "Ranch Market—Hollywood"; a cold, tenebrous ribbon of dead-straight highway dwindling to infinity in "U.S. 285, New Mexico"; a deathly automobile in a white shroud flanked by dark palm trees in "Covered Car—Long Beach, California." That pioneering hippie outfit, Ken Kesey's Merry Pranksters, converted a school bus in 1964 and made the coast-to-coast road trip the medium through which to taunt Middle America with a mobile spectacle of alternative behavior. "Counting the cars on the New Jersey Turnpike/ They've all gone to look for America," sang Simon and Garfunkel for melancholy sixties dreamers in Simon's song "America." Then, in a postscript for the postmodern 1980s, Albert Brooks gently laid the road trip paradigm to rest with his wistful and underrated little movie comedy *Lost in America*; in it a disaffected thirty-something, middle-class couple set off from California for New York in an all-mod-cons Winnebago, in search of a dream they ultimately discover that both they and America may have outlived.

Humbert and Lolita's trip has now taken its own place in the mythology of the Great American Road Trip, but still it is often characterized as biting satire even though neither Humbert nor Nabokov sought to denigrate the America behind the sometimes brash, commercial vulgarity of its roadside manners. Humbert and Lolita's tragedies are personal ones, not symbolic ones. Nabokov loved America and was distressed by those critics who saw malice or contempt in Humbert's ironic observations about their "lovely, trustful, dreamy, enormous country." Taylor Caldwell, for instance, praised *Lolita* but saw it as aiming its destructive fire at the "puerile materialistic and sickening fun of the perpetually adolescent American people."

If *Lolita*'s road trip has any spiritual cousins, they can be found neither in the political invective of Miller's prose nor in the morose beauty of Frank's intentionally bleak photographs but rather in the canon of film noir, where it was almost always personal tragedies that provided the impetus. Escaped prisoners, corrupt insurance salesmen, guys with a shady past they would rather forget—these are the unlikely partners in crime of urbane Humbert, the European aesthete criminalized by his sexual appetites. Accordingly, it is the stark neon signs, bright headlights, and prison-bar Venetian blinds to be seen in *They Live by Night*, *Double Indemnity*, or *Out of the Past* that are recalled in Lolita's road trip. The widescreen color landscapes that would characterize the next generation of Hollywood road-movie fugitives—Butch Cassidy and the Sundance Kid, Bonnie and Clyde, or Thelma and Louise—were something different again. But Humbert, possessing a much sharper sense of self-preservation than those particular road buddies (or indeed his own precursor in *Volshebnik*), had absolutely no plans to die in some romantic, no-compromise grand gesture. Like bank robber Bowie and country girl Keechie in Edward Anderson's 1937 classic hard-boiled novel *Thieves Like Us* (the basis of the movie *They Live by Night*), he wants to live—but sanctuary is always fated to be nothing more than a postponement of the day of reckoning. Roadrunner Humbert is only seeking to stretch the period of his dominion over Lolita into weeks and months, not years. Not only is there a realist behind the dreamer who knows his luck must run out, he also knows that any nymphet, by his own persnickety definition, can exist for only a limited period. Nine to fourteen are his strict age parameters, after which nymphets become merely conventional, earthbound young girls and of no interest. Lolita will turn thirteen halfway through their journey, a journey that despite its inexcusably base motive is not only one of the most evocative in American literature but also one that offers an interesting series of contrasts with another very famous and almost contemporaneous road trip.

Jack Kerouac's novel *On the Road* was put together and published at approximately the same time as Nabokov's *Lolita*. Both books were begun in 1950. Nabokov's was completed by the start of 1954 while Kerouac's would not be ready for press until 1957. Stylistically worlds apart, both novels ended up hitting the headlines in the United States at about the same time. The American publication of *Lolita* had been much delayed, having been rejected by a string of publishers—Viking, New Directions, Farrar Straus, and Doubleday—before Putnam's finally accepted it in 1958. (Roger W. Straus has claimed that he did indeed offer Nabokov a contract on condition that the author did not hide behind a pseudonym, something Nabokov had certainly thought of doing out of consideration for safeguarding his academic employment at Cornell.) Despite having taken longer to write, *On the Road* therefore preceded *Lolita* onto the nation's shelves by a few months. Kerouac's famous book conflated and lightly fictionalized the 1946 to 1950 real-life road trips undertaken by the author and his inspirational buddy Neal Cassady. (By revealing coincidence, Cassady's interest in an underage girl was one of the things that Kerouac's circumspect Viking Press editor Malcolm Cowley chose to excise from the manuscript.) Recasting Kerouac as Sal Paradise and Cassady as Dean Moriarty, *On the Road* expressed in loose, spontaneous prose all the excitement and adventure inherent in breaking the taboos of the day through a series of wild automobile trips dedicated to unrestrained indulgence in sex, drugs, and experimental spirituality. *Lolita*, by contrast, featured not only elegantly structured prose (the kind Kerouac and Cassady considered sterile) but also a more strategically considered itinerary, one that was designed to divert and restrain a child while camouflaging the sort of taboo breaking that even *On the Road*'s editor balked at seeing in print.

Humbert and Moriarty also drove rather different cars. In *On the Road* the automobile was utilitarian transportation. Usually in pretty bad shape and highly susceptible to breaking down, the car was simply a disposable means to an end. Its sudden failures might become part of the adventure, but otherwise the car itself was merely essential, not important. Humbert's automobile, on the other hand, became a worn but dependable coconspirator, the mechano-organic headquarters of his fugitive relationship with Lolita. In this respect Humbert's grand tour finds a further echo in those 1940s pulp fiction tales of private eyes and reformed criminals whose bachelor pads might be basic and characterless but whose automobiles fit them like a natural carapace that stored all of life's essentials—cigarettes, gun, whiskey bottle—within easy reach. Controlling Humbert and fractious Lolita also seem to be at home only in their car, which is the one constant environment they enjoy, if that is the word. In it they can fight and argue and bargain and make up with one another in their grotesque simulacrum of family life; the motel cabins change, but the car always stays the same. Long after Lolita has left Humbert, it is in the recesses of the car that painful souvenirs will turn up unbidden: a three-year-old bobby pin discovered in the depths of the glove compartment after he has found and lost Lolita for the last time filled Humbert with particularly acute pain.

Mexico provides the focus of the fourth adventure in *On the Road*, where it represents the ultimate road trip destination for Paradise and Moriarty. No less self-indulgent than Humbert, they cross the border in riotous style and spend a wild night with a roomful of prostitutes in a small village where an old Mexican woman sells marijuana from her backyard. Sal winds up with a bad fever and is promptly abandoned by Dean, whose sense of loyalty is rarely a match for his highly developed selfishness. For timid Humbert, on the other hand, Mexico is a temptation and a risk that in the end never becomes a reality. The road trip takes in Conception Park,

Texas, near the Mexican border that, Humbert says, he simply did not dare to cross at the time. (Lolita's own conception, we may recall, took place across this border.) When it comes to a second, shorter road trip still some turbulent months in the future, Humbert becomes bolder and begins toying with the idea of discreetly crossing that Mexican border, away from the past and into a Lolita-land well away from the gaze of the U.S. law. But in the end he never takes that outlaw trail and lives to regret it. The tacky Mexican honeymoon souvenirs that littered Charlotte's Ramsdale home remain a novelistic foreshadowing of a trip that neither Lolita nor Humbert will ever make. Conception Park remains the closest they will ever get, along with a few places in New Mexico where, incidentally, one of the tourist traps they visit is the phantom settlement of Shakespeare. Although it is to be found on no atlas, Shakespeare is not one of Humbert's or Nabokov's inventions but a genuine ghost town, the specter of one originally built on the site of an ambitious but unsuccessful nineteenth-century mining speculation. A ghost town on a phantom journey.

Well-read Humbert chooses to dub their touring car "Melmoth," referencing the itinerant hero of Charles Robert Maturin's Gothic novel *Melmoth the Wanderer*. Melmoth takes them all over the United States and ages plausibly in a period of history that follows a five-year moratorium on America's domestic production of automobiles, a hiatus imposed to divert industrial energies to the war effort. With no new vehicles to buy it was quite usual for 1940s cars to put in uncommonly long service with one owner, gradually becoming familiar, battered, and even anthropomorphized extensions of their occupants. "Hi, Melmoth, thanks a lot, old fellow," says Humbert in a fond valedictory gesture to the vehicle near the end of his memoir. A few weeks before, a rediscovered Lolita had less sentimentally observed that the superannuated vehicle was getting kind of purplish about the gills.

In its prime, Melmoth took Humbert and Lolita on a capricious cross-country route that, years later, Humbert's memory and a tattered collection of tour books could only approximate.

Prior to leaving New England in August 1947, quartermaster Humbert supplies his young mistress with a revealing cornucopia of consumer items that mirror her ambiguous child/lover status. These include comics, candy, clothes, a portable radio, a tennis racket, and some sanitary pads. Then, beginning with a few unexplained local meanderings, Humbert and Lolita drive through Virginia and the Carolinas down to Georgia, Alabama, Mississippi, and Louisiana, dallying in New Orleans and finally striking out west. Humbert's memoir, although geographically very vague, does contain many specific tourist attraction details that seem to suggest that, while never venturing northeast of Pennsylvania, they do dip into at least twenty-eight different states all told. They probably spend the winter in New Mexico and Arizona, then, reaching the Southern California coast via a looping detour through Nevada, strike out north as far as Oregon before slowly snaking back east, taking in South Dakota, Kansas, Missouri, Illinois, Indiana, and Kentucky, until they reach the college town of Beardsley a mere four hundred miles from their point of departure.

— — —

With the functional motel as his lodging of choice, Humbert entertains himself (and his reader) with his often waspish commentary on the names, decor, and peculiarities of these establishments in particular and America's commercial landscape in general. Lolita too is not slow to mock the more fanciful conceits of the hospitality trade, sneering at their tacky promises of raid-the-icebox snacks and horseback rides along moonlit trails. Yet an ineffable sadness surrounds her hankering after more substantial hotels and mock colonial inns, grand impersonations of family homes that promote themselves with promises of picture windows, friendly atmosphere, home cooking, informal snacks, and outdoor barbecues—simulacra of the home life that gypsy Lo no longer has and to which she can no longer realistically look forward. Yet even these hollow imitations of domesticity are absent from Humbert's preferred lodgings, those cellular, utilitarian, no-questions-asked motels.

Lolita is addicted to the gadgets that are attendant to their lifestyle—electric fans, coin-slot radios—as well as the omnipresent jukeboxes that demand to be fed with coins in each diner they visit. Despite Humbert's bored lack of interest in the American popular music of the day, we learn, by inference, that Lolita favors Jo Stafford, Tony Bennett, Sammy Kaye, Peggy Lee, Guy Mitchell, and Patti Page. This mix does not sit particularly well with Humbert's assertion that she likes "hot, sweet jazz"—these were, after all, mainstream pop musicians, several of whom had hits with smooth metropolitan versions of country songs. Although his loose grasp of genres is quite plausible, Humbert's boredom with popular music is frustrating; it would somehow have been nice to learn that Lolita sings along to, say, Patti Page's "Confess," and surely even Humbert himself might have found amusing traces of Little Carmen in Peggy Lee's cheerfully racist ditty "Mañana (Is Soon Enough for Me)," another jukebox favorite of 1948. We are also told that Lo likes square dancing (no hot, sweet jazz there either), although it is far from clear how Humbert's strict isolationist regime would allow her to participate in what at the time was essentially a couples community event usually organized by local dance clubs. Perhaps she simply admires square dancing as a spectator.

By contrast, Lolita's love of movies is something that Humbert can share, if only in a spirit of good-natured mockery of their clichés. This is just as well since over the course of the year on the road they see between one hundred fifty and two hundred movie programs as they hop from town to town, encountering as well many duplicated newsreels that cannot keep up with these moviegoers' fast-moving and prodigious cinema habit. (Today's younger film fans should bear in mind that before the days of TV news—and this road trip happened about five years before broadcast TV began in the United States—film newsreels routinely accompanied the features at the local picture show, striving to be topical but of course lagging far behind print and radio since the film had to be processed and physically distributed around the country.) As for the movies, as already noted, Lolita favors musicals, gangster films, and Westerns, but her insatiable hunger for the picture show is to wane as soon as their trip ends. It is replaced by a not altogether innocent obsession with the theater.

— — —

There is something rather poignant and revealing about Lolita's reading matter on the trip: just as Charlotte was in near-religious awe of those magazine arbiters of taste when it came to interior decor, Lolita is unquestioningly deferential to the teen etiquette wisdom dispensed in the movie-fan magazines she devours. She also uncritically accepts the press release wisdoms that accompany newspaper and magazine pinups, and, revealingly, her attention is always caught by photographs of weddings that appear in all the local papers they pick up on their travels. On one point she is immune to cajoling or threat: she will not squander her "vacation" time reading even the most accessible novels, and as a result *Little Women* (and was she herself not now a little woman?) and such will remain to her, quite literally, closed books.

Reinforcing Lolita's child status, Humbert is obliged to deploy the trick familiar to all exasperated parents on a long car trip, inventing or talking up focal points in the day ahead so as to give his fidgety and easily bored kid something to look forward to. As oblivious of the passing scenery as she is to their tour book's fulsome descriptions of areas of natural beauty, Lolita is nevertheless charmed by the bright signs of commerce: fancy logos and archly imaginative toilet signs, glowing jukeboxes, and the sacred imprimatur of a celebrity dining expert. Humbert also notes her enthusiasm for, among other things, the famous Burma Shave billboards, those strategically spaced sequences of ads along the 1940s highways, each with its calculated eighteen-second reading time for car occupants traveling at thirty-five miles per hour. Humbert references one specific Burma Shave sequence of word bites about a bearded lady, but, although he is a hirsute man who shaves both his face and chest, he does not mention—and so perhaps has not seen—the Burma Shave series that prefigures his own banal betrayal:

His cheek
Was rough
His chick vamoosed
And now she won't
Come home to roost

Fake dad and captive kid press on, hopping from tourist attraction to natural phenomenon in a giddy kaleidoscope of sightseeing gone mad: pueblo dwellings, a wine barrel–shaped church, Yellowstone Park, Mount Rushmore, a zoo in Indiana, a lighthouse in Missouri, Mission Dolores (!) in San Francisco, and some three hundred fifty nights in their different-but-the-same Pine Views, Green Acres, Hillcrest Courts, and Mountain Views. Later Humbert will recall an itinerary of around one hundred and fifty days of actual travel interleaved with two hundred days of standstills. All told he will spend around ten thousand dollars on their grim joyride.

— — —

Lolita is kept strategically lonely during the trip. At one point a statistically unlikely near-encounter with a vacationing Ramsdale family (the McCrystals) causes her to beseech Humbert to let her talk to them, something that suggests the kind of homesickness that no longer has any real point: her mother is dead and the Ramsdale home has been indefinitely let. Humbert does not relent. Her equally passionate appeals to pick up hitchhikers are also turned down. Her bids to spend leisure time with the kids of motel neighbors—a visit to a library, horseback riding, a roller skating rink—are frowned upon and, if grudgingly granted, chaperoned or else subjected to quasi-military surveillance by paranoid Humbert.

Nothing will dispel Humbert's fear that he will be found out. Even his enduring confidence in the anonymous privacy of the motel cabin proves misplaced when one night he discovers that their sexual activities must be clearly audible in the neighboring room from which there comes, too late, a clearly audible cough. Yet despite such reminders of the danger he courts, Humbert persists with their aimless tour as the seasons change and Lolita grows slowly more indifferent and then hostile toward him. On hot afternoons, Humbert tells the reader, he might recline naked in a leather armchair in the current motel room, with his miniature mistress sitting on his lap picking her nose and trolling the funny papers for the latest exploits of her favorite teenage cartoon character, Penny. Penny's name is not actually given but Humbert's precise description identifies her unmistakeably—and it seems that Lolita's enthusiasm is not a casual one. Popular Penny Pringle shared something of Lolita's circumstances, being the creation of a middle-aged man (cartoonist Harry Haenigsen had first conceived and drawn her in 1943 when he was forty-three) who bestowed upon her imaginative bobby-soxer slang that he kept fresh by eavesdropping at the soda fountains of his home town Lambertville, New Jersey. Nabokov similarly listened to schoolgirl conversations on buses, pouncing on what, even to a man with his prodigious linguistic skills, must sometimes have sounded like a wildly exotic patois. There is something touching about Lolita's enthusiasm for Penny, a self-assured adolescent of the 1940s with Katharine Hepburn cheekbones, a bevy of boyfriends, and a full complement of parents who were always supportive if frequently mystified by their daughter's escapades.

Humbert is less mystified than terrified by Lolita's potential responses to advances from boys. Significantly, the road trip is where we might reasonably look for the origins of Lolita's popular reputation as a teenage tramp, but we will look in vain. Despite the inevitable opportunities for lonely Lo to seek a beau (coffee shop, restroom stop, soda fountain, motel parking lot, tennis court), most suspected moments of treachery (as Humbert sees them) turn out to be cases of mistaken identity or imagined motive. When they are stopped for speeding by a cop, Humbert panics, but Lolita turns on the full charm because she has been conditioned to fear the law at least as much as he does. Her dimpled smile saves the day and may be considered the product of a sound strategic mind rather than evidence of an overly flirtatious nature, which is certainly how Humbert sees it. Humbert might also accuse her of coquetry when some amiable stranger accosts them and strikes up an innocent conversation about hometowns based on the evidence of their license plates, but he offers little objective evidence that his stepdaughter is any more of a tease than any other girl of her age.

We are not told much of Lolita's reactions to some of Humbert's more suspect excursions undertaken during the trip—for example, his failed bids to find a beach redolent of the one where he once fatefully failed to possess Annabel Leigh, or his attempts to realize with Lolita his unfulfilled fetish for possessing unattainable little girls in public parks. Now with his ideal nymphet in tow, Humbert finds it more difficult than he ever imagined to organize sex alfresco. After almost getting caught in the act on a secluded midsummer mountain trail, they beat a hasty retreat to Melmoth, with Lolita struggling into her clothes and, not for the first time, shocking Humbert with the colorful excesses of her language.

Humbert is the first to admit total ignorance about Lolita as a person. His sexual obsession is all that links him to a little girl about whose tastes and dreams he really knows nothing. Lolita remains a puzzle and a source of surprises until some notable incident—like the coitus interruptus above—reveals some aspect of her character that catches his attention. The road trip contains one such moment that not only reflects badly on Lolita but also demonstrates Nabokov's extraordinary talent for pulling off unexpected mood shifts. One day after Humbert and Lolita have joined a crowd of spectators staring at a blood-spattered car wreck with a young woman's shoe lying in a ditch nearby, Lolita casually observes "that was the exact type of moccasin I was trying to describe to that jerk in the store." For a moment she and her captor seem similarly self-absorbed, until you remember that she is still a child and the life she is living is both unreal and unsustainable. Humbert seems to come to the same conclusion and finally decides that he can no longer delay the education that may divert his increasingly bored, tearful, and hostile charge.

He decides to return east, to the town of Beardsley where he knows a man in the French department of a women's college at which he fancies he may research the complex official implications of his technical status as guardian, a legal conundrum he says varies from state to state—although in no federal territory is carnal knowledge assumed to be part of the surrogate parental remit. Also in Beardsley is a "sedate" girls school at which Lolita may continue her studies. As their Great American Road Trip draws to a close,

Lolita is thirteen years old, eight pounds heavier, two inches taller, sexually active, reluctantly accomplished at trading physical favors for treats, and well established in the habit of crying herself to sleep on a nightly basis.

[7]

TAKE ONE:

"How Did They Ever Make a Film of *Lolita*?"

THE 1962 FILM OF *LOLITA* WAS TO GIVE THE WORLD ITS FIRST PHYSICAL incarnation of Dolores Haze. There were some eight hundred applicants for the job, and sifting through them took producer James B. Harris and director Stanley Kubrick so long as to threaten to delay the start of shooting. Meanwhile, Vladimir Nabokov was vacillating about becoming involved in the reimagining of his own novel for the screen. Director Kubrick and producer Harris had bought the rights to the book from Nabokov for $150,000 (plus a share of the profits) in 1958, and their first attempt to get the author to write a screenplay had come in July 1959; it amounted to nothing. Although tempted, Nabokov turned them down after a discouraging meeting in Beverly Hills during which Kubrick's concern about censorship—a concern that was in the end to handicap the film considerably—prompted his suggestion that the screenplay might somehow imply at the end of the story that Humbert and Lolita had been secretly married all along. It was an absurd and unworthy idea, but the author's initial rejection of the screenwriting job stemmed not just from fears of this sort of compromise but from misgivings about his own role. A novelist, not a scenarist, Nabokov was the first to admit that he had comparatively little aptitude for writing for what he called the "talking" screen.

"I am no dramatist," Nabokov conceded in the introduction to his eventually published screenplay, going on to say that if he were he would be a tyrant who demanded control of every single detail of the production, from costumes to sets. He also regretfully allowed that he had always known that some toning down of the story for a film version would be inevitable. "One [cannot] deny that infinite fidelity may be an author's ideal but can prove a producer's ruin," he philosophically wrote.

Despite declining the initial offer, in late 1959 the chronically insomniac author had subsequently been amused to find himself idly cinematizing certain scenes from his novel in "a small nocturnal illumination." When, early in 1960, a renewed and improved offer with the promise of a freer hand came from Harris and Kubrick, he accepted. His fee was to be forty thousand dollars plus an additional thirty-five thousand if he received sole credit for the script.

On March 1, 1960, Nabokov met with Kubrick at Universal City to map out some scenes in "an amiable battle of suggestion and countersuggestion." Then on March 9, both men met the frontrunner for the all-important role of Lolita. She came in the shape of seventeen-year-old actress Tuesday Weld. Nabokov called her "a graceful ingénue but not my idea of Lolita." For once the novelist with a reputation for selecting the exact word to convey his precise shade of meaning had seemingly made a bad choice. Whatever else she was, Susan Ker Weld, initially nicknamed Tu-Tu, and later

Tuesday, was not ingenuous. She was born in New York in 1943 and her father died when she was three. Although the fascinatingly named Lothrop Motley Weld had come from a wealthy Boston family, his widow and three children were left with very little money after his death. Susan started working as a child model at an early age and soon became the family's sole breadwinner. At nine she suffered (she later claimed) a nervous breakdown, at ten she began smoking and drinking, at eleven she started to have sex, at twelve she acted on TV, and at thirteen she appeared in a small part in Hitchcock's movie *The Wrong Man*. She then attempted suicide after embarking on a series of disastrous affairs with a series of much older men, including forty-four-year-old Frank Sinatra; she was fourteen at the time of that relationship. Here—or so the cynic might think—was the perfect proto-Lolita, at seventeen already so sexually experienced that she might safely be considered immune to any further corruption if she impersonated Nabokov's nymphet. It turned out Weld herself felt much the same way but came to a different conclusion. "I didn't have to play Lolita," she claimed. "I was Lolita." So she turned Kubrick down, announced a move away from teen roles altogether, and went to study at the Actors Studio. She went on to have sexual liaisons with Elvis Presley, Albert Finney, Terence Stamp, George Hamilton, Gary Lockwood, and a number of other male actors considerably older than herself. Her movie career eventually turned out to be uneven and largely disappointing, even though she did earn some credit for appearing in a number of offbeat or risky movies. Among these were George Axelrod's bracing satire of teen culture *Lord Love a Duck* (1966) and Noel Black's chillingly effective *Pretty Poison* (1968), a kind of contemporary variant of Bonnie and Clyde in which Anthony Perkins's lethal sociopath proves no match for Weld's deceptively innocent-looking all-American high schooler. Eventually her career disintegrated, and despite a 1984 appearance in Serge

Leone's *Once Upon a Time in America*, Tuesday Weld is most usually remembered as a feisty, gap-toothed, 1960s teen sex kitten, a
living precursor of the popular Lolita stereotype. But what if she
had played Lolita, one wonders? Would her own wild young life
have fused with Lolita's fictional one to inject some authentic whiff
of sex and experience into the role? Or would things have turned
out much the same as they eventually did in Kubrick's film? We
cannot know, but it seems a pity that this always-interesting actress
was not the first to flesh out Lolita for the screen. She might have
been good.

Wild child Tuesday Weld looked like a shoo-in to play Lolita in
Kubrick's film version, but she turned it down. Later she played high
school teen Sue Ann Stepanek in *Pretty Poison*, where she turned out
to be the personification of the title. (*Pretty Poison*, 1968, 20th
Century Fox)

By September 25, 1960, the question of casting had been settled
without any further consultation with Nabokov. On that date, at
Kubrick's Beverly Hills house, the director showed the author some

photographs of Sue Lyon ("a demure nymphet of fourteen or so" was Nabokov's neutral verdict) whom, Kubrick assured him, could easily be made to look younger and grubbier for the part.

Lyon, born in 1946 in Davenport, Iowa, had been a child model for JCPenney in Los Angeles and had also played small parts in two 1950s TV shows, *Dennis the Menace* and the Loretta Young showcase series, *Letter to Loretta*. After Kubrick cast her, Lyon issued a conventional kind of Hollywood press release with a few innocuous details about herself: she was "just an ordinary, typical sort of grown-up American girl," she claimed, and playing Lolita, she felt certain, would not change her. As things turned out, it was an optimistic prediction. At fourteen, Sue Lyon had a pretty face and a shapely figure that combined to give her an intermittently adult look, albeit one so bland that Kubrick had felt the need to reassure Nabokov that this blonde teenager could somehow be dirtied up to resemble his tomboyish, chestnut-haired little girl. She never was, and in most scenes of the film she would look closer to twenty-one than twelve. To be charitable, perhaps the dress and makeup styles of the day—high heels, full skirts, cinch belts, curled and dyed hair—played their part in reinforcing Sue Lyon's rather mature on-screen image, although this theory is not helped by the difficulty most audiences might encounter in trying to determine exactly what "the day" might be. When exactly is Kubrick's *Lolita* set? The 1940s of the novel? Apparently not. The 1950s? The early 1960s? In terms of sexual behavior (and quite a lot of other things) these were very different decades, so it is extremely strange not to have the period clearly identified from the start. Kubrick's film looks strangely adrift in both time and space. While the novel was happy to "fictionalize" place-names as part of its conceit about protecting the innocent, the locales Nabokov created were all diligently observed, and in terms of geography and dates, the book is extremely precise and specific. Those scholars who have taken the trouble to deconstruct Humbert's many schedules and itineraries have found the novel's internal topography and calendar to be carefully planned; the few errors that do appear (the chief one being Humbert's erroneous claim about the exact number of days that have elapsed since he started writing his memoir—fifty-six, which is inconsistent with certain things the reader has already been told) are the exceptions that prove this general rule. Meanwhile, Nabokov's limpid prose brings a scientist's diligent observation to every detail, from the interior design of motel cabins and the weird and wonderful tourist attractions Humbert and Lolita visit to the commercial color charts of contemporary automobiles and the inflections of 1940s teenage slang.

In the course of the film it slowly emerges that Kubrick seems to have set the action about ten years later than the novel—although deducing even this much requires some distracting detective work on the part of the audience. The locations do not help. Apart from a few second unit shots of New Hampshire towns, a stretch of what looks like New Mexico desert, some library footage of U.S. highways, and general purpose back-projection material, the film was shot in Britain. More precisely, *Lolita* was shot in and around Elstree Studios a few miles north of London. Charlotte's white frame house (an authentic New England vernacular style) is impersonated by a mock-Tudor brick dwelling in the Buckinghamshire village of Gerrard's Cross, a short drive from Elstree Studios. In fact, all of the exteriors are 1960s suburban English streets halfheartedly tricked out with American street furniture and, in one instance, an implausible gas station. This results in the complete absence of any authentic sense of place. In another pragmatic ploy, Kubrick cast an informal repertory of expatriate Canadian supporting actors (Cec Linder, Lois Maxwell, Jerry Stovin, Shirley Douglas, Isabelle Lucas) and so introduced accents that, while not those of old England, hardly suggested New England either. Of course, such practices were not uncommon in low-budget movies of the time, but they were more likely to be seen in modest British supporting features than a high-profile MGM production. But if all this fakery was due to budget limitations or moral concern (legend had it that such an incendiary movie simply could not have been made in America at the time—an unproven and frankly unlikely contention), it remains Kubrick's willful evasiveness about the period in which the action is set that poses the greater puzzle. The embossed legend on the cover of Humbert's pivotal diary clearly reads "This Year" instead of an actual year (1947, we are specifically told in the novel). Lolita's begging letter to Humbert (seen in very close shot) is dated with the month and day, yet it too omits the year. Again, this looks like an intentional ploy to be vague. No authentic contemporary popular music is featured at any point in the film, despite Lolita's jukebox mania that Nabokov so lovingly addressed in the book—all that research into the names of late forties pop singers. All we get is a rather syrupy Nelson Riddle score, a vapid song, specially written and best forgotten ("There's No You"), and an insistent instrumental theme tune that rings out randomly from a radio, a band at the prom, and other places—music in a vacuum to match the ersatz locations. Inevitably, though, there are one or two period clues. Lolita plays with a hula hoop on the Ramsdale lawn (the hula hoop craze dates from 1957) and joins Charlotte and Humbert at a drive-in to watch the Hammer movie *The Curse of Frankenstein*, also 1957 vintage. On this evidence it seems we must conclude that the film's action takes place in the four-year span between 1957 and the year of the film's shooting, 1961. This decision to set it in "the present day" (the film starts in 1961 and then flashes back to 1957) seems odd, because while the novel is suffused with late 1940s period detail, Kubrick does not seem to have uprooted the action from that decade for any real purpose. Only the promotion (if it is a promotion) of Quilty from playwright to TV writer hints at any acknowledgment of a new time setting.

The film opens with the book's climax: Humbert's tragicomic murder of Quilty. We do not know why this urbane English-sounding man (James Mason) has come to a stranger's ornate and cluttered house to commit a murder, but commit it he does after a series of comic delaying tactics from his victim, played—overplayed, some would say—by Peter Sellers. Buying time, a drugged or drunk Quilty assumes the identity of Spartacus (a nod to Kubrick's previous film) while wearing a dust sheet as a toga and orchestrates a surreal, one-sided Ping-Pong match. He goes on to approximate the twangy accent of the archetypal old Western sidekick—a Gabby Hayes or a Walter Brennan—to read aloud an accusatory poem that Humbert hands him. The poem is a parody of T. S. Eliot's "Ash Wednesday," and this arcane literary touch, lifted from the novel, surely sits uncomfortably in a mainstream movie. Quilty then puts on boxing gloves and immediately takes them off again when Humbert begins firing his pistol in an unintentional echo of the amateurish marksmanship in the Western movies that he, Charlotte, and Lolita once sat through. Quilty goes on to pretend to compose a song at the piano before making a run for it and finally gets fatally shot while cowering behind a large framed reproduction of an eighteenth-century portrait of a woman. (The painting alludes to the logo of Gainsborough Pictures, a British B-movie outfit that in the 1940s turned out period melodramas often featuring the young James Mason as the suave villain.) A close-up of the bullet-riddled painting marks the end of a spirited opening sequence that nonetheless denies us any hint of the gory and surreal horror of Quilty's death as depicted in the book. Nabokov portrays him as an assassinated tyrant, a fallen king who is "bleeding majestically" in his slow retreat to the master bedroom, suddenly developing "a burst of royal purple" where his ear had been. Here his death is, literally, stylized out of sight.

After Quilty's killing, we flash back to Humbert's airplane arrival in the United States from Europe four years before and then pick up the forward trajectory of the novel from that point. Much has been omitted, some of it disatrously. We do not see or hear anything of Annabel Leigh, and we learn hardly anything at all about Humbert's lifelong obsession with nymphets. All we see is him arriving at Charlotte Haze's home in search of lodging and, as in the book, loathing it but suddenly changing his mind when he catches his first glimpse of Lolita on a beach blanket in the yard, a mock-seaside reference to the Annabel episode completely lost since the audience knows nothing about the kingdom by the sea. It is no exaggeration to say that the unprimed audience may at this point assume nothing more than that Humbert is partial to pretty teenage girls.

The famous movie still of Sue Lyon sunbathing is perhaps the best-known image from Kubrick's film. Reclining gracefully on her blanket, she actually looks not so much tomboyish as soigné. From her fancy perforated sun hat and her feline sunglasses to her two-piece swimsuit and long tapering legs, this is certainly no unwashed kid. This Lolita maintains a look of detached amusement as Humbert discreetly ogles her. She has with her on the blanket a couple of books, a ring binder, and a portable radio. Here she is at last: Lolita made flesh. What, contemporary audiences might have asked themselves, was all the fuss about? Sue Lyon simply looked like a slightly more sophisticated version of Sandra Dee, the blue-eyed blonde who, in her Gidget persona, was the epitome of naughty-but-nice late 1950s teen sex appeal. Certainly Kubrick had a vested interest in making his Lolita look as old as possible on the grounds that a teenager was less likely to fall foul of the Production Code Authority than might an ostensible twelve-year-old. In keeping with the general calculated vagueness of the film, however, Lolita's age is never actually given at all on-screen. Kubrick has been quoted as saying, wrongly, "I think that some people had the mental picture of a nine-year-old, but Lolita was twelve and a half in the book; Sue Lyon was thirteen." In point of fact, Sue Lyon was fourteen at the start of filming and fifteen at the end of it. In any case, the audience has only Lyon's physical appearance to go on, and Kubrick's promise to Nabokov that she could be made to look younger than her actual age seems to have been either forgotten or ineptly honored.

The critics, it should be said, did not immediately take to *Lolita*, the movie. In response to its rhetorical tagline "How did they ever make a movie out of *Lolita*?" the June 14, 1962, *New York Times* review supplied a neat and obvious answer: they didn't. Instead, "they made a movie from a script in which the characters have the same names as the characters in the book, the plot bears a resemblance to the original and some of the incidents are vaguely similar," Bosley Crowther wrote. "But the *Lolita* that Vladimir Nabokov wrote as a novel and the *Lolita* he wrote to be a film, directed by Stanley Kubrick, are two conspicuously different things."

Crowther went on to argue quite reasonably that Lyon's mature look effectively removed the factor of perverted desire and placed Humbert's passion on a par with that of innumerable older men who, in the history of the cinema, have pined for younger females without causing too much of a scandal. Perhaps surprisingly, the astringent critic Pauline Kael greatly admired the film, although she was already a Kubrick fan. But even she questioned Sue Lyon's squeaky-clean looks by dryly pointing out that girls of Lolita's age at her own daughter's school not only looked experienced, some of them actually looked badly used.

In truth, Nabokov can hardly be said to have written the finished film's screenplay at all, although he certainly wrote *a* screenplay, a version of which was eventually published in 1973. In it, following a much shorter version of Quilty's murder, a very long prologue takes us through various back stories: there is an address from psychiatrist Dr. John Ray, the supposed author of the novel's foreword; we see Humbert in his prison cell, beginning his memoirs; we are shown the childhood Humbert/Annabel Riviera episode; a montage of Humbert's encounters with various nymphets in Europe (little girls roller skating, playing marbles, doing calisthenics) is presented; Humbert's palliative marriage to a Russian woman in Paris and their subsequent breakup are shown in detail; we get Humbert's sea voyage (not plane trip) from Europe to New York; his library address to a women's club, in which his obsession with young girls is revealed and he suffers a nervous breakdown; and we see his admission to a "psychotherapeutic home" and the care of Dr. Ray, who prescribes a period of summer relaxation in the quiet New England town of Ramsdale, where the patient might lodge in a lakeside house belonging to the cousin of an acquaintance until he can take up a fall teaching appointment.

Knowing the difficulties Kubrick eventually experienced in faking a plausible Ramsdale in England, one can only smile at the alarm he must have felt upon being required by Nabokov's prologue to simulate the following: the French Riviera, Paris, a voyage into New York Harbor (Humbert, "Dramatically Standing on a Liner's Deck," sees "The towers of New York looming in the autumnal mist"), and a nursing home, a library, and assorted exteriors for the retrospective parade of European nymphets. Kubrick's solution was to cut the entire prologue and, after Quilty's murder, begin the story in flashback with Humbert's arrival at Charlotte's house four years earlier. In the process he also cut a scene showing the aftermath of the fire that destroyed Humbert's intended lodgings from which he was to be diverted to Charlotte's.

— — —

Nabokov, who regarded Kubrick as an artist, was initially very disappointed when he finally saw the movie that used only odd scraps of his screenplay (rumor has it that Kubrick and Calder Willingham cooked up the eventual screenplay between them, but Kubrick would never be drawn on the matter, and it was Nabokov who was nominated for an Oscar for best screenplay). In later years, Nabokov became more generous toward the film, still deploring some of its low spots and missteps, but feeling more inclined to consider it a "vivacious variant" of his book than a travesty. The film has always divided critics, however. Unpopular on its release, it gradually became critically rehabilitated as time passed, quite often being subtly reclassified as "a black comedy." Relieved of its contemporaneous burden of enacting a scandalous book, it seemed, by the 1980s, to be starting to be appreciated for its entertaining lead performances. Revisiting *Lolita* now, the viewer may find that Sue Lyon comes out of it rather well, delivering the best and least stagy performance, but the plaudits belatedly given to James Mason's Humbert, Shelley Winters's Charlotte, and Peter Sellers's Quilty seem more generous than accurate. Winters was certainly in top form as the overbearing, sexually frustrated, culturally pretentious Charlotte, but in the end her character comes over as nothing more than a grotesque at whom it is easy to laugh but about whom it is hard to care. Mason, meanwhile, is forced to underplay Humbert with a good deal of dry comedy, as if taking part in a dark sitcom. In the end his Humbert comes over as a good-looking but ineffectual rogue who suffers from occasional bouts of bad temper as he seeks to seduce a pretty teenager while living in a decidedly tense domestic situation. Once the brooding young villain of melodramas like *The Wicked Lady* and *The Seventh Veil*, Mason certainly retained an element of dangerous charm in middle age, but his is a Humbert lacking claws, fangs, and vitriol. Deprived of the novel's inner voice and hamstrung by a timid script, the actor cannot begin to hint at

Humbert's haunted past, his eviscerating humor, his awful sexual obsession, his calculating cruelty.

Peter Sellers's largely improvised appearances as Clare Quilty (appearing—in order—as Quilty himself, a police officer at a convention, a German psychoanalyst called Dr. Zemph, and an anonymous night caller on the phone) now look like a dry run for his multiple roles in Kubrick's next film, *Dr. Strangelove or: How I Learned to Stop Worrying and Love the Bomb*. Sellers's Quilty amounts to no more than a series of comic vignettes defined by quirky accents and extemporized dialog that recall his professional beginnings as a protean performer in *The Goon Show*, an iconoclastic British radio comedy series from the 1950s. There is little doubt that Kubrick's decision to give Quilty so much screen time and Sellers so little direction imbalances the film badly. A figure that should be a malign, shifting shadow keeps taking center stage and doing cabaret turns.

Throughout, Kubrick's treatment seems to be somewhat at odds with a literary source he so obviously admires. In addition to the staginess of the locales, the ambiguous time period, and the timid denial of the book's driving obsession, the look of the film is also oddly and unnecessarily unsympathetic to Nabokov's vision. This is strange because in his early feature, *Killer's Kiss*, former photographer Kubrick proved himself not only an adept student of film noir but also a budding filmmaker with an uncommonly good eye for locations. He shot *Killer's Kiss* himself on location in New York City in 1955, and although it obviously suffered from a very low budget and was forced to use largely unknown actors, most of whom were destined to stay that way, it does contain some fine visual material with bright, monochrome vérité footage of Times Square and dramatic waterfront skylines offsetting the mean warehouses and hotel room interiors. Kubrick explored film noir again in his next picture, the celebrated 1956 racetrack heist movie *The Killing*, and again seemed very much at home with it. It is a shame that he did not revisit the genre—even in a spirit of parody—for his treatment of *Lolita*, a novel that positively bristles with both literal and oblique references to such films (*Brute Force* and *Possessed*, both made in 1947, are name checked) and abounds with literary noir-ish effects. Instead, Kubrick's *Lolita* settles for the high-key lighting routinely used by MGM at the time so that what might have been a film of subtle visual suggestions and textures ends up being both overlit and overliteral.

What of Lolita's debut in the flesh? Sue Lyon manages to project a plausible blend of whining, pleading, wit, resentment, flirtation, and combative rebellion. That the dreadful heartlessness of her plight is never properly depicted deprives her of any emotional context, but that is hardly her fault. She really is very good at mood shifts: "Oh look, all the nines are changing into—" she begins brightly, looking at their car's odometer, only to be violently cut short by desperate Humbert, who is worried that a pursuing automobile, and with it retributive fate, are drawing ever closer. The exchange comes straight from the novel, and Lyon's startled response to Mason's curtness is just one example of her pleasing ability to react rather than act. Her brief 1950s TV apprenticeship seems to have prepared her well to give what is the film's only truly unaffected performance. Ironically, it is in such automobile sequences that she seems closest to Nabokov's Lolita—because it is those sequences that represent the film's most conspicuous betrayal of the book after its denial of pedophilia. Incredibly, the novel's epic road trip, that beautifully evoked yearlong, looping journey to nowhere that forms the centerpiece of the novel, is effectively omitted from the film altogether. Gone is the vast promise of the U.S. highways, the idiosyncrasies of the roadside lodgings, the elegant irony of a perpetually moving prison set in a limitless landscape, and the full rotation of the seasons through August 1947 to August

1948. It is replaced with two shorter trips, each with its own specific destination and each staged here in a series of static tableaux showing Lolita and Humbert sitting in their studio-bound car with only back-projected scenery for context. The first trip is from eastern summer camp to Idaho, where Beardsley College awaits them (the institution has been transplanted from its eastern location in the novel, presumably to enable this revised cinematic schedule); the second is from Beardsley to points south, in what Humbert believes to be a mutually agreed bid to escape to Mexico, although this trip has actually been surreptitiously proposed and stage-managed by Clare Quilty. Here, though, on Elstree's virtual road, Sue Lyon's Lolita is at her most plausible and sympathetic. The enclosure of the car, with both passengers in the shot, gives Lyon and Mason a chance to spark off each other at close quarters without distractions. Freed of those aging fashion accessories, Lyon even looks closer to her actual age as she sucks on a soda straw, chews gum, pulls faces, and alternates between bright acquiescence and whining protestation with a palette of expressions that ranges from diffuse prettiness to slack-mouthed vulgarity—probably a pretty good approximation of what Nabokov had in mind. But because we don't fully grasp that Mason's Humbert is a pedophile, we can only really see these scenes as conventional father/daughter sparring matches, not unlike those traditionally practiced on-screen by everyone from Spencer Tracy and Elizabeth Taylor to Ryan and Tatum O'Neal. This couple may be sharing motel bedrooms, but the audience might be forgiven for thinking that the most intimate thing that happens there is what was shown behind the film's opening credits: Humbert solicitously painting Lolita's toenails.

Stanley Kubrick's perennial defense of the absence of sex in his *Lolita* was that in the early 1960s censorship simply made it impossible to do justice to Nabokov's theme. His justification, often repeated and paraphrased, was "because of all the pressure over the Production Code and the Catholic Legion of Decency at the time, I believe I didn't sufficiently dramatize the erotic aspect of Humbert's relationship with Lolita. If I could do the film over again, I would have stressed the erotic component of their relationship with the same weight Nabokov did." Yet, as Elizabeth Power pointed out in her 1999 article "The Cinematic Art of Nympholepsy: Movie Star Culture as Loser Culture in Nabokov's *Lolita*," "Other contemporary and even earlier films suggest that Kubrick's placement of blame on censors is not particularly accurate or convincing." It is true to say that, by the 1960s, pedophilia was very occasionally starting to be acknowledged in mainstream films. Samuel Fuller's *The Naked Kiss* demonstrates the early difficulties of depicting it. A serious but wildly expressive filmmaker rarely given to understatement, Fuller has his heroine, reformed call girl Kelly (Constance Towers), discover her society fiancé molesting a little girl in his own home. The film deals with the moment of discovery so oddly that at first it is hard to understand what is going on. A little girl emerges from a corner of the living room and runs out dutifully as if to play. Only then do we see Kelly's grim-faced fiancé also emerging from the shadows. We are left to infer what was going on from Kelly's hysterical response, which involves clubbing and killing her intended with a heavy telephone. Awkwardly presented as the scene is, *The Naked Kiss* does at least try to address the hot issue head-on and, in doing so, is one of several films of the time to undermine Stanley Kubrick's routine defense of the complete absence of sex in his *Lolita* by citing the censor as an immovable force. *The Naked Kiss* was made in 1963 and released in 1964. Two years later, Kubrick's Lolita, actress Sue Lyon, would give a far sexier performance as a jailbait teen Charlotte Goodall to Richard Burton's disgraced preacher in John Huston's movie of Tennessee Williams's *The Night of the Iguana*.

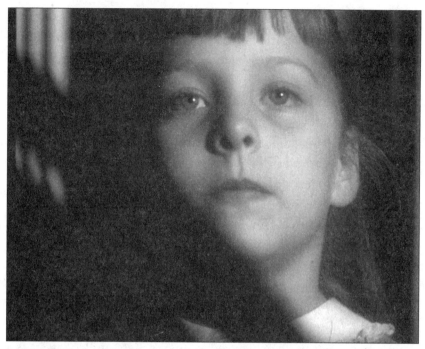

An unnamed little girl emerges from the shadows where a pedophile lurks in Samuel Fuller's melodramatic but bold movie *The Naked Kiss*. (*The Naked Kiss*, 1964, Allied Artists)

Taking a broader view of Kubrick's work, the director seemed to have a pathologically uneasy relationship with the forces of censorship, whether applied externally or, more usually, by himself. He effectively withdrew his own *Fear and Desire* (1953) from circulation by buying up all known prints. He blocked any rerelease of *A Clockwork Orange* (1971) in Britain after its initial showing there, allegedly because of fear of copycat crimes of violence; it was then not seen in Britain for thirty years and only reemerged after Kubrick's death. Despite scant evidence of undue censorial interference with any of his work prior to *Lolita*, he seemed hamstrung by worry about the censor even before the screenplay was written. His line seems to have been not that the censor demanded cuts but that he himself did not venture to risk a confrontation. A difficult and complex man, Kubrick has been the subject of many studies, but the rest of his odd movie career lies outside the orbit of this book. All that remains to be said of his involvement with *Lolita* is that filming it coincided with his permanent relocation from the United States to the UK where he lived, apparently in mortal fear of flying, for forty-two years until his death in 2002. His home, Childwickbury Manor in Hertfordshire, was not far from the faux streets of Ramsdale. In what Nabokov might have called a thoughtful Hegelian synthesis, Kubrick's final movie, the disastrous *Eyes Wide Shut*, involved the elaborate replication of Manhattan streets on the lot at Elstree Studios. This time it was rather more persuasively done.

Sue Lyon's was a grimmer story and one that carried several sad echoes of the character she so famously played, as well as paralleling the life of Tuesday Weld. At the June 13, 1962, New York premiere of the film, Lyon arrived at Loew's State on Broadway as a Lolita-themed celebrity, wearing the heart-shaped sunglasses that had featured only in the movie poster and brandishing a giant lollipop. She was still too young to be admitted to the actual public screening. Ten years later her life was a mess. It emerged that even the innocuous press release she had issued on getting the part had been a lie—this normal American girl had come from a deeply troubled background. Now she claimed her mother had driven her father to suicide when she was just ten months old. Penniless, they took in lodgers, one of whom tried to rape eight-year-old Sue at knifepoint. She first had sex at the age of twelve, became a model, and at seventeen entered into the first of four marriages. She was diagnosed as bipolar and put it all down to *Lolita*. Sue Lyon may have been dramatizing and transferring blame for her bad luck, bad judgment, or bad behavior, but then again she may not. In the days when she still talked about her Lolita experience at all she said, "I defy any pretty girl who is rocketed to world stardom at fifteen in a sex-nymphet role to stay on the level path thereafter." By the time Adrian Lyne's film of *Lolita* came out in 1997, Lyon, it seems, could no longer even consider the dreaded name rationally. "I am appalled they should revive the film that caused my destruction as a person," she told Reuter's news agency in a by now rare public statement. Lyne's film would be no revival, it would be a completely fresh cinema treatment of the novel, but Lyon was beyond such distinctions in her hatred of Lolita, the poisonous name of her nemesis.

As a postscript to Kubrick's film, it seems appropriate to mention what we might call a close cinematic relation of *Lolita*. The first film ever directed by the legendary French director Louis Malle was a lighthearted attempt to cinematize a novel that was arguably even more unfilmable than *Lolita*. The book *Zazie dans le métro*, as mentioned in chapter 3, was written by Raymond Queneau, who greatly admired Nabokov's *Lolita* and gave his own child heroine her looks as well as her mix of innocence and cheerful vulgarity. Visiting Paris, provincial Zazie wants nothing more than to ride the metro of the title, the city's subway system, but it is immobilized by a strike. So she shakes off her dubious guardian, a female-impersonator uncle, and explores Paris on foot. The book makes playful use of phonetically spelled French slang, much of it vulgar, in an episodic, literary tale that Malle's 1960 color movie recast as a fast-moving farce with silent movie gags and Road Runner references instead of the linguistic allusions. Malle cast young Catherine Demongeot as Zazie. Demongeot, it has to be said, would have made the perfect Lolita: twelve years old, chestnut hair, slangy speech, mischievous and rebellious, she is also sexually neutral in a way that means any middle-aged man shown to be attracted to her would be immediately identified by his singular craving and not excused as having a more conventional appetite for pretty young girls. Demongeot (who would jokily reprise her Zazie role in Jean-Luc Godard's *Une femme est une femme* one year later) is perhaps the ideal screen Lolita who never was.

Catherine Demongeot in *Zazie dans le métro*, the film of Raymond Queneau's tour de force novel. Queneau greatly admired *Lolita*, while Demongeot bore more than a passing resemblance to Nabokov's description of his heroine. (*Zazie dans le métro*, I960, Nouvelles Éditions de Films)

It would be thirty-five years before the next movie of *Lolita* appeared. In that period the *Lolita* brand would take off in a giddying multiplicity of directions. Yet the enduring irony of Stanley Kubrick's film was that it in no way added to the popular myth of Lolita as promiscuous seductive teen. Whatever its merits or faults, one thing is unarguable: there was simply no sex at all in Stanley Kubrick's film of *Lolita*. Expectation had outrun what the product delivered. A *New Yorker* cartoon from 1962 has a man and his wife emerging from a showing of *Lolita*; he is saying, "How could I enjoy it with that woman behind me saying 'tch, tch, tch' all the time?" One wonders what the woman behind him disapproved of. A further irony: a complete absence of sex was one of the few criticisms that could not be leveled at Lolita's next two incarnations, both of which would be on the stage. A legendary lyricist felt he could do justice to the story in a musical setting, and then one of America's leading playwrights took it on himself to pay his own theatrical tribute to Nabokov's heroine. Subsequently, each might have had grounds for joining with Sue Lyon in identifying Lolita as a force for evil.

[8]

DRAMATIC ARTS:
Lolita Center Stage

THE NOVEL *LOLITA*, HEAVILY DEPENDENT ON A NARRATOR'S INTERnal monologue, does not seem to lend itself well to stage presentation—even less so than film presentation, which leaves open the possibility of voice-over. It does present one advantage over a film treatment, however: the cinema's troubling demand that only a little girl can plausibly play Lolita is potentially eased. ("It was perfectly all right for me to imagine a twelve-year-old Lolita," Nabokov had said prior to Kubrick's film. "She existed only in my head. But to make a real twelve-year-old play such a part would be sinful and immoral, and I would never consent to it.") Without close-ups, a theatrical performance does not necessarily need a very young girl, just one who can play young; this freedom also makes the later depiction of a seventeen-year-old Lolita a lot easier. (One of the few times Sue Lyon did not look too old as Lolita was when she donned glasses and stomach padding as married and pregnant Lolita, at which point she looked too young.) The first attempt to put Lolita onstage, however, did not take advantage of this option with regard to age. It was one misjudgment among many in what was to become a resounding commercial (if not an artistic) disaster. Helmed by talented people, this venture was doomed to fail before it began. It was *Lolita*, the musical.

Lyricist Alan Jay Lerner was a Harvard-educated man, a student friend of John F. Kennedy who had progressed through Harvard's Hasty Pudding musicals to become a writer of continuity scripts for the long-running NBC/CBS radio show *Your Hit Parade*. After a chance meeting with Austrian composer Frederick Loewe, Lerner became his lyricist, and the pair went on to write some spectacularly successful musicals that included *Brigadoon*, *Paint Your Wagon*, and one of Broadway's all-time hit shows, *My Fair Lady*. When the partnership finally ended and Loewe retired, Lerner sought other musical partners including Burton Lane and Leonard Bernstein, but he was never to repeat the success of the Lerner-Loewe partnership.

Coco (1969), a short-lived musical about the founder of the House of Chanel cowritten by Lerner and André Previn, was followed two years later by an alliance with another musician, the successful British movie composer John Barry. Their musical show was to be called *Lolita, My Love*.

Nabokov had only been persuaded to give his approval to the project because, as in the case of Stanley Kubrick, he was always sympathetic to those whom he considered serious artists even when he knew little about their chosen medium. Nabokov had already demonstrated, with his elephantine screenplay for *Lolita*, that he had no real idea how films were written, let alone made; now his often-admitted lack of appreciation for music disqualified him from assessing anything but Lerner's impressive track record of writing intelligent, literate musical books. "If you have to make a musical version of *Lolita*," said Nabokov, whom one suspects could see no such need in the first place, "he is the one to do it."

– – –

The Broadway venue was to be the Mark Hellinger Theatre on West 51st Street, a previously lucky theater for Lerner where *My Fair Lady* had triumphed. The director was Tito Capobianco, who had made his New York City Opera debut in 1965 with *Les Contes d'Hoffmann* to considerable acclaim. Richard Burton turned down the role of Humbert, so British Shakespearean actor John Neville (much later of *The X-Files*) was cast in the key role. Dorothy Loudon (a durable Broadway comedienne) played Charlotte. *Lolita, My Love* tried out in Philadelphia in February 1971. The reviews were so bad that producer Norman Twain closed immediately for a complete overhaul. Annette Ferra, the fifteen-year-old originally cast to play Lolita, was replaced. They would try out again in Boston, premiering at the Shubert Theatre on March 15, 1971, for an intended run of three weeks. The cast now included a new Lolita, thirteen-year-old Denise Nickerson. Tito Capobianco had resigned and been replaced by Noel Willman. Choreographer Danny Daniels (who had replaced Jack Cole during rehearsals) was himself replaced by Dan Siretta. The revamped show won some qualified plaudits from the critics in Boston, mainly for Lerner's lyrics and John Neville's Humbert, a portrayal apparently distinguished not only by a good performance but also by a strong vocal contribution. Dorothy Loudon's Charlotte was colorful enough to be sorely missed when she died at the end of the first act. The public, however, did not really miss her because they never came in the first place. *Lolita, My Love* closed after only nine poorly attended performances and never made it to New York. It did not even spawn a legitimate cast recording, although rehearsal tapes were made, an album cover was printed, and some vinyl discs pressed. The show lost $900,000.

What remains of *Lolita, My Love*? The poor quality audio recording, probably taken from the soundboard during rehearsals, still exists. A handful of commercial rerecordings of some of the show's less obviously expository songs have surfaced over the years by MOR vocalists including Robert Goulet and Shirley Bassey. John Barry's own instrumental recording of the theme, *Lolita*, was—perhaps defiantly—included on an album called *The Very Best of John Barry*. The bootleg cast recording album sleeve lists all of the show's songs, and some of them provide a tantalizing shorthand summary of what comprised *Lolita, My Love*:

"Going, Going, Gone"
"In the Broken Promise Land of Fifteen"
"Dante, Petrarch, and Poe"
"Sur Les Quais"
"Charlotte's Letter"
"Farewell, Little Dream"
"At the Bed-D-By Motel"
"Tell Me, Tell Me"
"Buckin' for Beardsley/Beardsley School for Girls"
"March Out of My Life"
"All You Can Do Is Tell Me You Love Me"
"How Far Is It to the Next Town?"

It is diverting to think that, had things gone differently in Boston, "Dante, Petrarch, and Poe" might have been become as familiar an entry in the Alan Jay Lerner songbook as "On the Street Where You Live" or "I Was Born Under a Wandering Star." In the end, though, *Lolita, My Love* disappeared into the well-populated Hall of Shame of failed musicals, along with the now-legendary *Carrie*, a musical version of the Stephen King/Brian de Palma horror-fest that faithfully included the film version's opening shower room scene in which Carrie is taunted for being terrified by the onset of her first period. Yet there is good reason to believe that *Lolita, My Love* had merits that lifted it above many of its fellow failures. Musicals maven Ken Mandelbaum has written that "Lerner's lyrics were frequently dazzling, and Barry's music indicated genuine talent as a theatre composer only hinted at in his other stage scores. 'In the Broken Promise Land of Fifteen' for Humbert, a showstopper for Loudon called 'Sur Les Quais,' a nightmarish, cross-country sequence called 'How Far Is It to the Next Town?' and most of the other songs demonstrate how well Lerner and Barry succeeded in musicalizing the characters."

Perhaps, after all, the show was as good as it could have been, but the faulty foundation upon which it was built was the assumption that the public was ready for a musical about a child molester. The presence of a thirteen-year-old leading lady probably made it an even more distasteful prospect for its presumed audience. Denise Nickerson would have turned fourteen in the role in April 1971 had the run lasted that long; as it was, the opening number, "Going, Going, Gone" became its swan song. A happy-ending footnote was that, in contrast to Sue Lyon's experience, the Curse of Lolita did not ruin Denise Nickerson's life; after a good run in film and TV (including a stint on *The Brady Bunch*), she moved to Colorado and became an accountant. In the same year *Lolita, My Love* flopped she also appeared in the film *Willie Wonka & the Chocolate Factory* and was thus fondly remembered by a whole generation not as a sexualized child in a musical but as Violet Beauregarde, the gum-snapping kid who turns into a blueberry in Roald Dahl's famous morality tale.

Lolita, My Love did little harm to John Barry, whose movie career continued to flourish and who to date has won five Academy Awards and four Grammys. It did, however, clearly mark the beginning of the end for the estimable Alan Jay Lerner. *Coco* had not done particularly well, but *Lolita, My Love* was the first of five decisive flops. Somehow his luck had changed; he turned down an offer to write the English lyrics for *Les Misérables* and was about to start work on the lyrics for *The Phantom of the Opera* when he died in 1986. It was a bitter end for a talented man who had once had the

Midas touch; Lerner would not, however, be the last well-regarded artist to have his reputation blighted by Lolita.

In 2005, playwright Edward Albee wrote, "Vladimir Nabokov's *Lolita* is a book I have admired greatly for a long time, and when I adapted it to the stage I was determined to render its excellencies— its dark humors, its heartbreaking pathos—intact to the stage." His adaptation would come a decade later than *Lolita, My Love,* four years after Vladimir Nabokov's death, and was of course this time to be a nonmusical play. This was the early 1980s, when Albee already enjoyed a considerable reputation as the playwright who had reenergized the American stage with his domestic take on the theater of the absurd as pioneered by European playwrights like Eugène Ionesco and Samuel Beckett and further advanced by Harold Pinter and Tom Stoppard. Albee's body of work already included *The Zoo Story* (1959), *The American Dream* (1961), and *Who's Afraid of Virginia Woolf?* (1962), so his reputation seemed secure, and few had demurred when he was dubbed one of the few genuinely great living American dramatists.

Albee's *Lolita* made its debut at the Brooks Atkinson Theatre in New York City on March 19, 1981, almost exactly ten years to the day after *Lolita, My Love* folded in Boston. The casting contained one slight Nabokovian irony: this time Lolita was played by twenty-five-year-old Blanche Baker, whose mother, Carroll Baker—at about the same age—had played Tennessee Williams's Baby Doll Meighan. Donald Sutherland, the Canadian movie star who had not acted on stage for seventeen years but who could offer an approximation of the British accent he mastered during his extended 1960s sojourn in London, was Humbert Humbert. The physically imposing actress Shirley Stoler was a roly-poly Charlotte. Urbane Scottish actor Ian Richardson was cast as A Certain Gentleman, a kind of onstage authorial presence. It might have been interesting. Instead, it was a total disaster.

Retracing the texture of an ephemeral event like a theatrical performance over a quarter of a century later is not an exact science. We have the reviews (in this case universally damning), but we cannot revisit what they were reviewing. We do, however, have Albee's published play, presently included in volume 3 of his collected works. A caveat from the author suggests that, as with most of his plays, he has, in new collections, tweaked a few things with the benefit of hindsight. (This was a liberty upon which Nabokov would have frowned; once the piece was written, that was it as far as he was concerned—it was time to burn the rough drafts and alternative versions and move on.) On the page, Albee's *Lolita* is compelling only in its awkwardness. Its most daring device is that of introducing a detached authorial voice, embodied by the character of A Certain Gentleman who provides an ironic, Olympian commentary on the proceedings, often bantering with exasperated Humbert (who is given to complaining about the way the action is turning out and even the quality of the writing) and generally reminding the audience that this story has a puppeteer for an author. This is a strangely dated 1960s device redolent of those fleetingly modish TV plays that would reveal the camera crew to remind the audience that it was watching a TV play, or new-wave movies like Jean-Luc Godard's *Le Mépris*, where the mechanics of moviemaking self-consciously intrude at every turn. Even so, to begin with A Certain Gentlemen at least promises to give expression to the authorial voice so lacking in other enactments of *Lolita*.

To summarize the play: to the accompaniment of dry banter between the narrator and Humbert, it begins with Humbert clutching a life-size doll (which he futilely begs the narrator to explain), who is briefly joined by Lolita herself clutching a doll of her own. This Lolita is eleven years old ("Eleven and a half!" she insists), and already we get a glimpse of the Haze household in front of which long-dead Annabel appears in order to allow Humbert to explain the source of his obsession with little girls. In flashback we see Humbert's arrival as a potential lodger at Charlotte's home, mocking the plastic ivy framing the exterior of the front door and vowing never to move in there. (The plastic ivy business troubled at least one reviewer of the Broadway production who thought Albee was already mocking the artificiality of the play itself.)

Events proceed roughly as in the novel, although Humbert's interjections as a self-appointed critic of the play keep intruding. Humbert obliquely mocks the author's decision to give Annabel a surname that so obviously evokes Poe's doomed heroine; he finds the device of Charlotte coming upon Humbert's incriminating diary corny. ("How could you!?" he asks A Certain Gentleman— who replies, "Plots must turn on something.") Lolita bouncing on Humbert's lap was apparently enacted with much writhing and groaning from Humbert onstage, although as written in Albee's latest version of the play it is forestalled by a domestic diversion, and Humbert graphically describes the procedure to the audience. Charlotte dies not in a car accident but by falling down stairs while attempting to shoot Humbert with her first husband's pistol. There is a protracted funeral gathering, then, when Humbert collects Lolita and they go to their first motel (no Enchanted Hunters here), the action coarsens abruptly and illogically. Humbert is outspoken about his lust and his plan to render Lolita compliantly unconscious by means of a drug: "I shall hold her kidskin buttocks in my rough, large hands, and I shall lift her toward me, her downy mound at my nostrils, at my mouth," he announces to the narrator, who is faintly embarrassed, as well he might be. Lolita, for her part, seems only too aware of Humbert's ambitions to have sex with her and is apparently quite happy to oblige without any need for sleeping pills or pretext. Fresh from the shower, she stands in her robe facing Humbert with her back to the audience and her arms spread wide ("See Tiny Alice," says Albee's stage note in a strange self-regarding reference to the crucifixion scene in his own 1964 play of that name). The robe falls, Lolita is naked onstage, and her popular reputation as a brazen tramp is further advanced. The plot grinds on, more or less faithful to the letter of the novel but missing its bittersweet spirit entirely; fellatio and cunnilingus are simulated; the epic road trip (now meaninglessly inflated to five hundred days) is included but can only be suggested by fragmented scenes in stylized motel rooms; Clare Quilty is represented in a manner that apes Peter Sellers's disruptive chameleonic turns in Kubrick's movie; Lolita leaves, Humbert grieves, and the play ends as does the book with Quilty's murder and Lolita's death in childbirth. Albee adds a final twist of the knife in the form of a confidence from A Certain Gentleman, who tells Humbert that Lolita's premature son actually survived for an hour or two and that her husband Dick named the child after him; unfortunately, deaf Dick always mistakenly believed Humbert to have been Lolita's natural father, so the doomed child is called Harold. Curtain.

"No one who saw the execrable production the play received on Broadway could penetrate through to the homage I was paying to Nabokov," wrote Albee in a 2005 introduction to the play.

After a troubled tryout in Boston, the production had certainly run into financial and artistic difficulties even before opening in New York. Sutherland and Albee quarreled, producer Jerry Sherlock ran into cash flow problems that resulted in Sutherland's first check bouncing, and further unwanted publicity came from a sixty-strong contingent of the activist group Women Against Pornography (WAP) waving placards saying things like Incest Isn't Sexy and Rape Isn't Funny.

"What we are protesting," announced WAP's Barbara Mehrhof, "is not just *Lolita* but the whole concept of the Lolita syndrome: the sexualizing of little girls. It's the whole Brooke Shields phenomenon."

Walter Kerr, reviewing the production for the *New York Times*, noted, "There is no sense of a genuine relationship—passionate, frustrated, or whatever—between Humbert Humbert and his little lass who is sometimes seen licking heart-shaped red lollipops. Lolita herself is virtually an unwritten character: in the entire first half of the evening she exchanges almost no words with her paramour." Kerr was the critic baffled by Humbert's drawing attention to the plastic ivy, a device he found typically dislocating. "Is he criticizing the stage setting for being unreal?" Kerr asked. "Is he saying that the owner of the house has tacked up plastic vines around her outside door? . . . That would be silly . . . since vines are so inexpensive and so easily trained. Is he saying that all growing things look like plastic to him? We don't really know what point he means to make, only that both Mr. Richardson and the greenery are elements detaching us from any sense of real life."

Time's T. E. Kalem was also unimpressed. "Albee took a technical gamble—and lost. He introduces a character called A Certain Gentleman (Ian Richardson) to share the burden of narration. Because the gentleman is supposedly Nabokov, Humbert Humbert's moral turpitude is diminished: he cannot, after all, defy the will of his creator. . . . (Blanche) Baker, chosen after a long talent hunt for prepubescent sexpots, is disappointing as Lolita. She begins as a little girl with a lollipop and swiftly becomes a brat with a staff sergeant's mouth and no trace of dreamy allure."

Dmitri Nabokov (who, too late, was appalled that he and his mother had ever been inveigled into signing a three-part contract that not only authorized Albee's play but also any future movie or opera based on it on condition that the play ran for at least fourteen days) later wrote, "From the day we received the play script with 'Enjoy!' scrawled on the cover by Sherlock, my mother and I were astounded by how grotesquely bad it was."

Sherlock kept Albee's *Lolita* going for the required minimum period and then it closed, probably to everyone's relief.

Stephen Bottoms, in his introduction to *The Cambridge Companion to Edward Albee,* places *Lolita* centrally in the period of Albee's perceived decline in the early 1980s. "*The Lady from Dubuque* (1980), *Lolita* (1981) adapted from Nabokov's novel, and *The Man Who Had Three Arms* (1983) were all assaulted with a ferocity out of all proportion to whatever crimes against taste or dramaturgy they may have committed," he wrote. "Albee, it seemed, was now yesterday's man, a remnant of the 1960s completely out of place in the new, Reaganite 1980s."

The film based on Albee's play was never made, although the contract held good and Albee's camp actually collected on Adrian Lyne's 1997 film that bore absolutely no relation to Albee's drama. The intended opera, slated to be cowritten by Leonard Bernstein, also failed to materialize after the drubbing the play received. Eventually, however, another opera did surface, this time rather unexpectedly in the Swedish language. Having seen how Alan Jay Lerner and Edward Albee fared, one might have expected Rodion Schedrin to demur, but late in 1994 the Russian composer premiered his four-hour opera of *Lolita* at Stockholm's Royal Opera. Due to another wrangle with the Nabokov estate (Schedrin had written the libretto but neglected to secure the rights), it was not possible to perform it in Russian or English, so it was translated into Swedish. There were eight Stockholm performances spread across December 1994 and January 1995, and critics found little to admire in Schedrin's words or music, although soprano Lisa Gustaffson's portrayal of Lolita was praised, as was the production in general and John Conklin's boldly stylized stage design, replete with imaginative icons, symbols and logos of 1950s America. For the record, the rest of the credits were as follows: director, Ann-Margret Pettersson; conductor, Mstislav Rostropovich; Humbert Humbert, Per-Arne Wahlgren; Quilty, Björn Haugan. In *Time*'s review Michael Walsh concluded that "Schedrin's lazy, impotent score is loutish when it is not downright sullen," and he too found praise only for Lisa Gustaffson. "She becomes the much younger, equally alluring sister of such operatic sirens as Carmen, Lulu and Katerina Ismailova. If only, like them, she had something to sing."

These extreme examples of dramatic disaster would seem to suggest that no sane person would ever again try to put *Lolita* on the stage. Yet it is in the nature of theater to revive and rework past failures to see if it was the times or something more intrinsic that defeated them first time around. Every now and again experimental productions of Albee's *Lolita* surface to test the contemporary moral temperature or just to try new interpretations. In 1999, the one hundredth anniversary of Nabokov's birth, the International Theatre Workshop tackled it at Lower Manhattan's Gene Frankel Theatre. In the opinion of Zembla, an admirable Web site for Nabokov fans, Russian director Slava Stepnov's vision of *Lolita* here was "less about sex and pedophilia than . . . about being a slave to one's own ego." Scotland's Edinburgh Festival has seen occasional bids to remake the story for the stage; Act Provocateur International once rendered it with a voice-over to point up the book's authorial voice. A 2003 Oxford University student version also produced for Edinburgh was adapted by Aidan Elliott and had Lolita "clambering all over Humbert with an offensive and almost comical lack of subtlety" according to one critic.

An Australian opera of *Lolita* was proposed by Melbourne composer Douglas Knehans in the mid-1980s, but he later thought better of it. In 2005, the Boston Symphony performed local composer John Harbison's overture to *his* proposed opera based on *Lolita*. The overture, however, was as far as Harbison ever got, since a local Catholic child abuse scandal erupted and threatened the spirit of dark comedy he had originally intended for the work. It is not recorded whether Harbison knew of *Lolita, My Love*'s ignominious collapse in Boston, but he eventually concluded that *Lolita* simply could not work in operatic form at all. Dmitri Nabokov has praised a "truly fine" Milan theatrical production of *Lolita* by Luigi Ronconi that was based not on Albee's play but on Stephen Schiff's screenplay for Adrian Lyne's 1997 film. "Let Albee & co. try to sue me," observed Dmitri Nabokov grimly, "but they're not getting a cent from that."

The Lolita Haze who emerges from all of these varied dramatic ventures seems most usually to have been either invisible or crass. Overcome by the weight of the production or a sense of occasion, it seems that few theatrical Lolitas have possessed the tenderness and the eerie, vulgar charm of the Lolita of the novel. Instead, we tend to glimpse either a kid almost completely hidden by the shadows of adult obsession or an exhibitionist adolescent with "a staff sergeant's mouth." Served so poorly by serious men of the theater like Lerner and Albee, how on earth would the poor girl fare in her emergent role as a brand name for underage sex and provocation in the cheerfully amoral world of popular culture?

[9]

THE SPIRIT OF FREE ENTERPRISE:
Every Foul Poster

ONE OF THE INTRINSIC DELIGHTS OF *LOLITA* THE NOVEL IS THE constant interplay between the "high culture" tastes of Humbert and the "low culture" enthusiasms of Lolita. Simply put, Humbert loves art for art's sake while Lolita hungrily embraces the infinite promises of commerce. Humbert's cultural world always takes into account Lolita's more limited one, but hers can never accommodate his. Perhaps, though, their two spheres are not always as far apart as we might imagine; Humbert and Lolita are, after all, both peculiarly susceptible to what we might very loosely call poetry, be it highbrow or lowbrow. Is Humbert's appreciation for the verse of Edgar Allan Poe any more passionately felt than Lolita's fondness for the syncopated rhymes of her favorite song, "Little Carmen"? Early in their relationship it is the differences separating them rather than the tastes uniting them that we tend to notice. She devours comic books and magazine stories but resists all of Humbert's attempts to introduce her to anything more "improving," rejecting even Gene Stratton Porter's accessible homespun novel, *A Girl of the Limberlost,* as too highbrow. Lolita's mother before her had also placed complete trust in the wisdom of magazine sages, her solemn appreciation of "culture" being in fact little more than a dutiful awareness of modish opinions gleaned from the same source and recycled at book club meetings and other small-town cultural gatherings. Lolita, although too young to be socially aspirational in that particular way, does seem to have inherited her mother's touching trust in the heady promises of lifestyle magazines and adds an insatiable consumer's appetite for the dreams such magazines promote. America's golden period of consumerism might still be two or three years in the future, but even during the relative austerity of the late 1940s, the constant allure of consumer goods and services is already a potent force in Lolita's young life. Modern kids usually want the same toys, clothes, and gadgets that their friends have, but Lolita's constrained circumstances meant that she did not even have friends for much of her meager childhood. During Lolita's year on the road her only steady companions come in the form of magazine story heroines, agony aunts, and disembodied radio voices. When they finally stop traveling, Humbert still discourages friends and vets the very few who get at all close to Lolita. This gives a poignant edge to Lolita's addiction to clothes, sweetmeats, diner food, movie idols, and popular music—experiences to share with the friends she never quite makes in the parody of childhood that Humbert has engineered for her. But even Humbert is forced to show grudging admiration when he records the heartfelt sincerity of her consuming passion for all manner of products and promotions, fads and fancies. For Lolita this sort of passion is never once matched by the promises of even the most populist art. In Stanley Kubrick's film, this particular point is rather well made when Humbert tries to read Lolita some of Edgar Allan Poe's poem "Ulalume." She responds to Humbert's lovingly savored articulation of the poem with a good-natured but dismissive, "Well, I think it's a little corny, to tell you the truth"—this from the kid who will go into instant raptures over the tritest billboard promise, unquestioningly buying the message that has been so pragmatically wrought and so accurately targeted.

When G. K. Chesterton saw the lights of Broadway for the first time, he observed, "How beautiful it would be for someone who could not read." Humbert's response to the brash heraldry of commerce that studs the 1940s American landscape is not altogether dissimilar. Yet despite his occasional outburst about "foul" posters, he chooses to treat everything he encounters in the American landscape, both natural and artificial, as a potential source of aesthetic pleasure and diversion. He is certainly not immune to the seduction of commerce even as he mocks the crassness of its impulse. Faced with his umpteenth Main Street USA one bleak night soon after Lolita has left him, he notes the pulsing and glowing signs of its stores and responds to them as beguiling unnatural phenomena that trigger in him visual and verbal associations just as a mountain or a fountain might. He records a camera shop's "sherry-red" illuminated sign, an effulgent green clock swimming in "the linenish depths" of a laundry, a garage whose prosaic sign for Gulflex Lubrication his overassociative brain at first misreads as "genuflexion lubricity."

"There is a touch of the mythological and the enchanted in those large stores," Humbert says of the establishment where he shopped for little girl clothes prior to abducting Lolita from school (noting, in passing, the shop assistant's talent for converting his technically precise requests into the appropriate commercial lingo: petite for small, and so on). While reflecting on his "poetical" afternoon of fussy shopping, he recalls the equally poetical name of a discreet hotel that dead Charlotte had once mentioned: The Enchanted Hunters. No more or less artificially marketed than any brand of soda, chewing gum, or burger, the as yet unseen hotel nevertheless strikes a visceral chord in Humbert; its name's echoes of pursuit and magic spells somehow appeal irresistibly to him, and, knowingly duped, he still likes the sound of it and wants to go there. Less sophisticated Lolita, that ideal consumer, meanwhile responds in a less self-aware but otherwise similar way to the blandishments of brand names and product descriptions that seem to promise her exactly what she wants. Rachel Bowlby, in her essay "Lolita and the Poetry of Advertising," writes: "It is Lolita who is the poetic reader, indifferent to things in themselves and entranced by the words that shape them into the image of a desire that consumption then perfectly satisfies. Appearing under the sign of 'novelties and souvenirs,' anything can be transmuted . . . into an object of interest, worth attention."

– – –

Lolita herself was eventually to become an enduring object of interest to the commercial world for reasons that were rarely literary. Her notoriety would eventually seep into every facet of commerce and fashion, ranging from sex toys and movie promotions to paintings and photographic art. It all began with that 1962 movie poster featuring a stylized Lolita sucking a scarlet lollipop and peeping over the lenses of sunglasses equipped with red heart-shaped frames. Her flirty gaze is contained, top and bottom, by the out-of-focus horizontals of a car window frame (although these were sometimes airbrushed out in the innumerable variants used for international posters and paperback book covers). Fashion photographer Bert Stern, who took the picture, seems to have toyed with the idea of making Sue Lyon into an adolescent Marilyn Monroe, an aim more obvious in another color shot from the same sessions. In it, Lyon's heavily lipsticked pout is much in evidence along with, again, the heart-shaped glasses; and again too she is in a car, shot through the window. But this time instead of playing the coy underage temptress, Lyon has been posed in a more overtly abandoned attitude, arching her neck back over the car seat and aiming her artificially plump scarlet pout at the camera lens à la Marilyn. At the time, Stern was already fascinated by Monroe, of whom he would soon take some twenty-five hundred photographs in a three-day session shortly before she died in 1962. As for the *Lolita* publicity shots, there were at least two rather more appropriate pictures taken by Bert Stern at the Sue Lyon movie poster sessions. (They were appropriate, that is, to the spirit of Nabokov's *Lolita* if not necessarily to the commercial ambitions of MGM, whose Humbertian Latin slogan—Ars Gratia Artis [Art for Art's Sake] sounds, in the case of Kubrick's film, a bit hollow.) One such photograph shows a scowling Sue Lyon—sans sunglasses, lollipop, and lipstick—slouched with her head lying sideways on her arm, which is resting on a car, a paper American flag held slackly aloft by the fingers of her right hand and with what looks like the sun hat she wears in the film pushed back off her head. Behind her is an out-of-focus storefront. Far less stylized than Stern's more famous shot of her, this was probably an informal "between-takes" picture. Although it is visually a little cluttered and ambiguous, it somehow captures a certain scruffy schoolgirl indolence that is entirely absent from Stern's other pictures, and indeed from the Sue Lyon of the film. Another shot shows a wide-eyed Lyon without makeup, looking extremely young, one hand holding back her hair, her face partially obscured by the reflection of sun-dappled trees in a car windshield or some other screen that lies between her and Stern's lens. It is a lovely photograph in which blue-eyed, yellow-sweatered Lyon looks innocent and vulnerable in a way she never would in the hard black-and-white cinematography of the movie being promoted. Of course, in the end it was the arch lollipop/sunglasses shot that would become iconic, and, as already noted, Lyon fitted herself out with similar props for the film's premiere. After the movie was released, Nabokov's Hollywood agent, Irving Lazar, came across some actual white-framed sunglasses with heart-shaped lenses and sent them to the Nabokovs as a gift. They were delighted, and there is a 1966 photograph of Véra Nabokov wearing them poolside at the Montreux Palace, the hotel at which the Nabokovs could afford to live for life following *Lolita*'s great success. Those same sunglasses were displayed in a case in the New York Public Library a few summers ago as part of a Nabokov exhibition; it was somehow rather affecting to note that one hinged arm had been broken and informally repaired. Also on display were first editions of *Lolita*, the index cards on which Nabokov always wrote his books in longhand, letters, and butterfly sketches. All of these things were predictable literary exhibits, but those glasses commemorated what? The start of the process of Lolita's corruption? Life imitating commercial art? The first time that Lolita, despite Nabokov's expressed wishes, was impersonated by a real girl?

Noël Coward's observation about the potency of cheap music perhaps applies equally well to the power of cheap graphic design, which the *Lolita* movie poster certainly was, even if its execution was superficially stylish. It established a visual symbol that stayed in the collective mind. By 1981, the New York production of Edward Albee's play had its Lolita sucking on a heart-shaped lollipop, a conflation of two phony props neither of which had been devised by Lolita's original creator but by a fashion photographer. Just as Baby Doll Meighan's shortie nightdress had become a generic product, heart-shaped glasses and other items were to become a loose trademark vaguely suggestive of very young, sexually available girls. In this way a counterfeit Lolita fashion was founded upon an accessory that had nothing whatever to do with the Lolita that Nabokov had realized in such precise detail and diligently accoutred with all those faded blue jeans, plaid shirts, tartan skirts, gingham frocks, and sneakers. Worse was to come.

Nabokov was still alive when, to his amused revulsion, life-size Lolita sex dolls first became available, fully equipped with the appropriate apertures. Now, in the twenty-first century, the Bratz range of sexy, Barbie-with-attitude dolls for girls is rarely discussed without some passing reference to Lolita. "The company behind Bratz sees its decision to bring 'hooker chic' into the bedroom of preteens not as 'premature sexualization', but simply an untapped commercial opportunity," wrote Tess Stimson in the UK's conservative *Daily Mail* newspaper in 2006. "There is a world of difference between harmless role play and Lolita precocity."

On the same theme, in a 2002 *New Statesman* article bemoaning the sexualization of children, Cristina Odone wrote, "Pre-teen has become an erotic term in itself; Lolita, a concept as familiar as Barbie." Both commentators took the view that targeting very young girls was mainly a commercial decision undertaken by companies who were running out of female teenage consumers and who saw not only an immediate impressionable preteen market to exploit but also a valuable recruitment platform for tomorrow's teenage customers.

In the intervening years, the Lolita name has been pressed into service to sell all kinds of objects, as well as justify a number of dubious artistic projects that seem to trade on the ambiguity of the blurred line between art and pornography. It has also lent itself to fashion styles and trends as far removed from 1940s Ramsdale as Mars or Venus.

In 1980, ex-*Pretty Baby* Brooke Shields appeared in press and TV ads for Calvin Klein jeans. The TV commercial (banned by broadcaster CBS) included the now fifteen-year-old veteran of many child pornography disputes delivering the tagline, "Do you wanna know what comes between me and my Calvins? Nothing." When

Women Against Pornography was railing against Edward Albee's *Lolita* play the following year, they were only one of many groups to lump together *Lolita* and Brooke as evidence of the sexualizing of little girls.

Not all who appeared to cash in on Lolita as a sexy brand name have been quite so nakedly commercial in their motives as the hawkers of life-size sex toys or accessories for young girls. If not all of them were the lofty artists they claimed, neither were they all necessarily immoral hucksters or outright pornographers.

British artist Graham Ovenden's series of Lolita paintings and prints from the mid-1970s caused a minor scandal when they were first exhibited, but they were defended as art rather than pornography, just as Nabokov's book had been—although in this case perhaps with less demonstrable justification. A vague adherence to certain locales of the novel (*Lolita at the Lake,* for example) and Ovenden's obvious skill as a draftsman could not change the fact that his artfully undraped Lolita owed rather more to some Pre-Raphaelite erotic stereotype (long luxuriant hair, a fey self-absorption) than to Dolores Haze. Some of Ovenden's other works, such as those depicting Lewis Carroll's Alice or five seminude contemporary girl children only identified by their first names, seemed to reinforce a legitimate suspicion that a graphic talent and the fame of others were being used to legitimize a personal obsession. Another Briton, David Hamilton, also courted controversy in the 1970s with his numerous soft-focus nude photographic studies of girls in their early teens. Despite a credible early career as a 1960s fashion photographer for *Vogue, Elle,* and other upscale glossy magazines, Hamilton always remained a suspect cultural figure in the United States and Britain, and his reputation was not helped when he directed a clutch of soft-core porn movies of which *Bilitis* (1977) remains the best known. *Lolita* was often brought into the Hamilton pornography debate not because of any actual link but because in the minds of critics Lolita's name was by now pretty much established as shorthand for any debate about smut dressed as art.

New York City–born photographer Jock Sturges has also faced repeated charges that his work was child pornography masquerading as fine art. In 1990, his studio was raided by the FBI, who confiscated much of his work and equipment. The offending images were of children of both sexes, most of whom were characterized by their nakedness, their physical beauty, and the kind of untroubled, eyes-straight-to-the-camera gaze that in itself seemed to be challenging and confrontational to the forces of conservatism. Christian groups protested as Christian groups will, civil liberties groups reacted, and Sturges attempted to defend himself publicly in talks and media interviews. Many of his images were certainly of very young girls, and in their studied informality, it could be argued that they were hardly any less contrived than Charles Dodgson's Victorian tableaux. The difference was that these were pictures of modern young girls who were growing up in a knowing culture of sophisticated magazines, movies, and TV commercials, the beneficiaries of late twentieth-century health care and nutrition posing naked on the recognizable beaches of west coast America or France. Without the distancing effect of yesterday's technology and dated visual manners—dubious excuses to be sure—to some this looked like conceited pornography. To others it was a celebration of the female body's beauty at its most striking. After a year, that FBI raid resulted in a grand jury throwing out the child pornography case. The public trial of a photographer, who had been born in the year of Lolita's Great Road Trip, had given a new generation, too young to remember the public outcries about Nabokov's novel, a minor child pornography debate of its own.

Sally Mann's photographs incited similar divisions in the late 1980s, particularly with her second published collection of pictures, *At Twelve: Portraits of Young Women*. Her images of twelve-year-old girls were more artful than Sturges's and unsettlingly echoed some of the techniques, if not the motivation, of pornography. Occasionally cropping her subjects in ways that might invite the charge of fetishizing certain body parts, *At Twelve: Portraits of Young Women* seemed to up the ante by going out of its way to draw attention to the blurriness of the line between childhood and adulthood, innocence and experience, pornography and art. When her next collection turned the lens on her own children, it caused a new outcry. *Immediate Family* (1992) contained what *Art in America* critic Ken Johnson called "luminously beautiful black-and-white images of mysteriously elfin children," while other observers considered it further evidence of Mann's fondness for sexualizing children, now with a suspicion of incest thrown in. Lolita's name was once again evoked by critics and intellectuals discussing Mann's pictures, and a 1999 exhibition of her work at the University of Virginia's Bayly Art Museum also included various accompanying wall texts, including some from Lewis Carroll and Vladimir Nabokov. A review in the university's weekly news magazine, *The Declaration*, by Jessie Blundell exemplified the kind of reaction that was almost guaranteed by bringing together three such disparate figures.

"Surprisingly, among the voices enshrined in text I found Nabokov and Lewis Carroll," wrote Blundell, who by her own admission had been emotionally disturbed by some of the pictures. "Their words read like personal insults, outrageously inappropriate, an impervious and mocking presence. While sophisticated literary theory may suggest veiled but benevolent motives, I find it impossible to escape Nabokov's creation. Like the photographic fantasies of pornography, he uses text to create scenes and stories; Nabokov calls pedophilia into being, writing life into both victim and offender, girl and man. And his story suggests that the molestation of girls results in some sexy self-sufficiency in women. Sexual assault remains flat and pathetic, one-dimensional in its influence, while survivors emerge reborn, all the better for the abuse."

As an aside, Blundell mentions that she "never made it through *Lolita*"—an extraordinary admission under the circumstances. So, a modest university exhibition probably prompted as much by Mann's local connections as her artistic reputation (she was born in Lexington, Virginia) threw up a revealing example of how *Lolita*'s bad press is not confined to the tabloids. The exhibition's strange curatorial conflation of a Victorian child fancier who wrote a famous children's book, a Russian American novelist whose public statements left no doubt as to his personal moral stance on pedophilia, and a photographer who intentionally flirted with the ambiguity of picturing naked children on the brink of adolescence betrays little understanding of any of those components, throwing them together in a particularly uncomfortable bed. A fair-minded reviewer might have disentangled this cultural muddle, but Blundell (who does not let the fact that she never even read all of *Lolita* prevent her from offering the absurd assertion that its author concluded that the molestation of girls turns them into sexy, self-sufficient women) simply co-opts Mann's images as an excuse to air her own feelings about child abuse. Her review is worth dwelling on only because it is typical of many responses to this particular subject. When it comes to discussions of child abuse, sociological or artistic, there always seems to be people for whom the very idea is so incendiary that they cannot wait to begin with their own moral conclusion and then work backward to try to make the facts support it. They always seem content never to have read the book or seen the movie or play that is central to the debate; moral certainty, it seems, makes the gathering of supporting evidence unnecessary.

— — —

Two views of Gothic Lolita. The Western book is a photographic cata-
log of young Japanese girls simply posing in their extravagant costumes. The Japanese magazine, aimed at the home market, integrates
the Loligoth look into a richly textured fashion world of pastel
stickers, badges, coupons, and international graphic references.
(Cover of *Gothic & Lolita*, Phaidon; cover of *Gothic & Lolita Bible*,
Index Magazines)

One of Lolita's more high-profile instances of commercial fame has
come from having her name adopted by a Japanese youth fashion.
Lolita Fashion in general connotes a frilly fantasy in which Japanese teen or preteen girls dress in a wildly stylized approximation
of Western Victorian or Edwardian girls, often complete with lacy
parasol, teddy bear, and Little Bo Peep hat or frilly headdress—
Alice Liddell on LSD. More famous still is the Lolita Fashion sub-
category Elegant Lolita Gothic, usually shortened to Lolita Gothic,
ELG, Loligoth or GothLoli. Extrapolating conclusions from all of
this is inherently problematic, since delving into Japanese popular

culture at all is fraught with pitfalls for most Western commentators. It seems even the most innocent assumptions about shared societal values cannot be made when it comes to Japan. In the present context it may be plausibly argued that Japan actually sanctions, or at least broadly tolerates, a national male obsession with schoolgirls. The sexual politics of the Japanese Gothic Lolita phenomenon is therefore something of a minefield.

What does seem clear is that for Japan, as for the United States and many other countries, the basic schoolgirl "look" is a particularly potent entry in the canon of male-oriented erotica or pornography. In Japan that look has been traditionally based on a school uniform of the sailor *fuku* style (white blouse, blue collar, red tie, short blue pleated skirt), although an auxiliary range of fetishized school outfits also exists in the various forms of navy blue one-piece swimsuits, gym clothes comprising tight white top and navy blue tights, and schoolgirl variants of traditional Japanese martial art clothing. On the face of it, this would seem to be comparable to American male fantasy fetishes for schoolgirl, Girl Scout, or cheerleader outfits. Yet in Japan the Lolita Gothic fashion phenomenon—which might at first be considered nothing more than another variant of the school-age girl fantasy—is also part of modern Japanese youth's own fondness for Visual Kei and CosPlay, role-playing that uses elaborate costumes, hairstyles, and makeup to create fantasy personae.

Attracting boys as well as girls, Visual Kei finds a distant Western echo in the British glam rock era of the 1970s, a movement that spawned David Bowie, Queen, and Roxy Music. It was mainly androgynous-looking males who dominated, but the symbiosis between the music and the elaborate theatrical costumes adopted by performers and fans alike seems to prefigure Visual Kei. Certainly there has been a Japanese rock music connection in the form of bands such as Rentrer en Soi and MUCC, who adopted role-model outfits to inspire their fans to imitate and compete.

By being part of the Visual Kei movement, Lolita Fashion and Lolita Gothic have therefore come to represent a particular form of self-expression for young Japanese girls that seems poised between the traditional role-playing of Kabuki and the elaborate sartorial confection of the geisha, which—at least in the form of *oiran* geisha—has clear associations with prostitution. So here is a stylized hybrid movement of rebellion and self-expression based on an image that seems to derive from a Japanese male erotic stereotype and is therefore overloaded with cultural and sexual references that leave journalists groping for plausible sound-bite descriptions. French maid meets Alice in Wonderland. Shirley Temple meets Morticia Addams. Victorian frills with glam rock platform shoes. Baby Doll as a Black Sabbath groupie. No words can quite do justice to the impact of Japanese Lolita Gothic, not least because it very much depends upon whom it is having an impact. Lolita Gothic has been adopted by young Japanese women whose slight physiques tend to evoke childlike or even doll-like associations—although these associations tend to exist mainly in the minds of Westerners. In Japan, Lolita Gothic is a different deal, and as a fashion it has never traveled particularly well. Courtney Love, in her early days with alternative rock band Hole, was occasionally hailed as the first bona fide American Loligoth, but despite her contrived look of depraved innocence, achieved through torn baby doll dresses and makeup that looked as if it had been applied by a nine-year-old with little mirror experience, Love was no elfin Japanese girl, so the overall effect came out rather differently.

Yet Lolita Gothic has been successfully exported through other media, ever since it seeped into the iconography of Japanese manga (comic and newspaper cartoons), anime (animation), and *bishōjo* (a type of video game based on interaction with stylized young girls depicted in the styles of manga and anime). All of these media trade in variants of the Lolicon (and how Nabokov, the lover of portmanteau words, would have squirmed to hear that one), the Lolicon being a sexually explicit graphic depiction of a stylized prepubescent girl character. The traditional Lolicon has huge eyes, a preteen physique, skimpy clothes, and some (usually) pastel accessories of childhood (hair in beribboned bunches and bangs, popsicles, toys, and so on). Gothic Lolita has already made its mark in these media, trading pastel colors for black-and-white lace collars and bows, headdresses, more tomboyish hairstyles, and a rather un-Victorian proclivity for producing death-dealing automatic rifles at moments of conflict. Gothic Lolicons also sometimes sport prominent bows on the front of their costumes, perhaps referencing the key sartorial distinction between geisha and *oiran*, the latter advertising their sex-for-sale status by wearing the obi at the front, not at the back as traditional geishas do. *Bishōjo*, the video medium, has met with most resistance to export because of the overtly sexual and sometimes pornographic nature of the player's possible interaction with the characters. Manga and anime, usually more mainstream, have therefore been the leading channels by which this particular life of Lolita has become well known outside of Japan.

What does the Loligoth phenomenon add to the sum of misunderstandings that have accumulated around Lolita's name? If in Japan its resonances are singularly domestic, in the West it has perhaps vaguely reinforced the idea of Lolita as a proactive coconspirator in her own exploitation. The spectacle of young girls publicly affecting costumes that contrive to blend the childlike with the enticing—and doing it, however unconsciously, in Lolita's name—only strengthens the general suspicion that somehow Dolores Haze was asking for it. It is an unworthy but widespread suspicion and one that finds its logical conclusion in the ultimate commercialization of Lolita's name: the Internet trade in pornography where three trips of the tongue down the palate—Lo-Lee-Ta—signify the sexual exploitation of underage girls who are often coerced to simulate

enjoyment of their ordeal. In a sense, this has been Lolita's final
ordeal, her last seduction—the traducing of the name of a rather
conventional, flirty little girl to indicate the availability of pornography that no one pretends is art.

The Lolicon connotes a subgenre of Japanese illustration where
childlike female characters are depicted in an overtly sexualized
manner. Often shocking to Western audiences, such characters seem
to exist less controversially in the unfathomable sexual landscape
of Japan. (Promotional poster for *The Lolita Girls Collection* by
Hikari Hayashibara, Ex Comics)

The world of Internet Lolitas is in fact a rather more complex
one than it may seem at first glance. As with everything else, the
Internet has complicated traditional perceptions of how information is delivered and received. In the precomputer days when Lolita
was first conjured into being in Nabokov's neat hand on a series of

index cards (an analog cut-and-paste system of the author's own devising), trafficking in pornographic material of any sort was still a comparatively risky business for both supplier and consumer, involving shady bookshops, mail-order services, and the black market. As a movie like *Hard Candy* demonstrates, by 2006 Internet pornography had bred sophisticated new protocols involving grooming and impersonation, bringing with them new generations of clued-up children and adults as well as a highly efficient transglobal distribution channel so complex that policing it has been reduced to a series of high-profile law enforcement gestures rather than any real control. It is a far cry from those distant days in Paris when disenchanted hunter Humbert, after responding to an ad in a dirty magazine, was led to an unappealing girl of fifteen or more with token braids and ribbons and, as further unreliable evidence of extreme youth, a threadbare doll. It is further still from the late nineteenth century, when the distribution of erotic postcards of children was largely limited to private collections that provided a model, but not yet a distribution channel, for the commercial production and consumption of child pornography. In a hundred years or so, this trade, having grown steadily at first, at last simply exploded.

By the early 1970s, much of Western Europe was taking a far more liberal attitude toward pornography, the trend being led by Denmark, which, in 1969, had legalized the production of all kinds of erotic material. The earliest child pornography movies were marketed under the name "Lolita" and were made by a Copenhagen-based company called Color Climax. It is estimated that a minimum of thirty-six ten-minute films were produced under this catchall title between 1971 and 1979. Pornographic magazine spin-offs drew upon these movies for still photographs. The "Lolita" films featured young girls, typically between the ages of seven and eleven, being sexually abused mainly, but not exclusively, by men. Meanwhile, in the United States, the commercial production and distribution of child pornography also began to flourish in a parallel climate of (comparatively) lax national law enforcement, often with linkups to European producers, sharing material and sometimes even sending images from the United States to Europe for initial publication prior to importing the resulting magazines. Amsterdam became the hub of this publishing trade, and it featured material with names that included Lollitots, Lolita Color Specials, and Randy Lolitas.

In their diligent book *Child Pornography: An Internet Crime,* Ethel Quayle and Max Taylor cite the case of Joseph Francis Henry, who testified to the Permanent Subcommittee on Governmental Affairs before the U.S. Senate, Ninety-Ninth Congress, February 21, 1985. Henry had been involved in the sexual abuse of twenty-two young girls, and in his testimony he described how domestic child abuse images were routed from the United States to the Netherlands. "Various motels and homes of two men were used as locations for the molestation," Henry testified. "The children were also photographed during sessions with the men. Although I did not participate in this, one of the men, I can't be sure which, apparently sold photos to the Dutch child porn magazine *Lolita* because in the *Lolita* issues 29, 30, and 31, there were shots of Tammy and Yvonne in various explicit poses."

Tammy and Yvonne, to whom one's heart goes out, may yet be reluctant porn stars. One of the more grotesque by-products of today's Internet distribution of child pornography is that a large proportion of it actually dates from twenty or thirty years ago, those old movies and still images now having been digitized. Quayle and Taylor claim that such vintage material is "by far the largest element of current child pornography available." For those abused children who are still alive, those filmed episodes from their grim childhoods are still being efficiently cataloged and sold. Quayle and Taylor note that "the various *Lolita* videos and magazines are identified as LL followed by the series numbers 1 to 36. A picture called LL23-30 therefore refers to the thirtieth picture scanned from Lolita video number 23."

Perhaps this is a good point at which to recall that in 1949 Quilty throws out adoring Lolita because she flatly refuses to participate in his pornographic movies. "I said no, I'm just not going to [blow] your beastly boys, because I want only you," Lolita tells Humbert at their last meeting, explaining why Quilty dumped her.

Denied a voice when Humbert first possessed her, this time she at least had a choice in the matter, and she said no. With that in mind, it seems doubly ironic that her name has since been bestowed upon generations of abused girl children who never had the option to turn down their enforced moments of stardom in front of the camera. Of course, had Lolita's name remained the fairly common Spanish diminutive it had been before Nabokov bestowed fantastic fame upon it, the pornographers would simply have found another generic label to identify their images of molested and beaten kids. But perhaps it is grimly fitting that those traders in abuse should have knocked off a name so mellifluous and rich in associations, since the theft is appropriate to the practice it describes: the stealing of childhoods to realize dark adult fantasies. In her most shameful corruption, Dolores Haze, alias Lolita, was reduced to a logotype for salable images of child abuse in progress, images old and new, color and monochrome, digitized and cloned, and now available on a computer screen near you.

[10]

TABLOIDS AND FACTOIDS:
The Press and Lolita

THE WORD "TABLOID" CONNOTES THE KIND OF NEWSPAPER WHERE everything—format and content—is compressed for the sake of convenience. It is often assumed that the term refers primarily to the compact size of the publication, yet the word—probably derived from the late nineteenth-century innovation of compacting pharmaceuticals into tablets—seems to have preceded the small-sheet format and was originally coined to describe the compressed, simple style of journalistic writing that made complicated issues easier to grasp by omitting digressions and shades of meaning. Tabloids in the United States date from the launch of the *New York Daily News* in 1919, a paper today locked in rivalry with the *New York Post*, which, under the ownership of Rupert Murdoch's News Corporation, has taken on many of the characteristics of the famously cutthroat British tabloids. In fact, tabloids originated in Britain, flourishing under the guidance of Alfred Harmsworth who, at the end of the nineteenth century, made a fortune by turning around failing newspapers, giving them a smaller format and making them more accessible. A slightly earlier publication, however, had shown the way and, in the course of its colorful history, also demonstrated that a populist newspaper could have a moral sense too—and one that concerned an issue central to *Lolita*.

The *Pall Mall Gazette* was founded in London in February 1865 by Frederick Greenwood and George Smith and began as an interesting example of life imitating art. It was the actualization of a fictitious paper dreamed up by William Makepeace Thackeray for his 1850 novel *The History of Pendennis*. That novel explored Thackeray's favorite theme of the green but ambitious youngster on the make, an idea he also used in *Vanity Fair* and *The Luck of Barry Lyndon*. The real-life *Gazette*'s original tone had been unashamedly elitist, fully in keeping with Thackeray's editorial prescription (the *Pall Mall Gazette* would be "written by gentlemen for gentlemen," Pall Mall being a London street famous for its exclusive gentlemen's clubs). In 1880, however, the actual *Gazette* passed from conservative to liberal ownership, and between 1883 and 1889, under editor William Thomas Stead, it became a vigorous campaigning newspaper. The fully illustrated publication now covered human interest stories and became much more accessible, featuring banner headlines and short paragraphs. Traditionalists deplored what they saw as the degradation of news journalism, and there was particular resistance to Stead's fondness for "the interview," a journalistic innovation that, a rival complained, indiscriminately gave voice to any "politician, religionist, social reformer, man of science, artist, tradesman, rogue, [or] madman" whose ramblings might offer titillation to readers.

Then in 1883 the *Pall Mall Gazette* published a series of articles on the subject of child prostitution, a practice that it labeled "the white slave trade." Sales of the paper increased from eight to twelve thousand. Two years later, Stead joined with Josephine Butler and

Florence Booth of the Salvation Army for an exposé of child prostitution that was to represent the *Gazette*'s finest hour. In July 1885, Stead arranged the purchase, for a sum of around eight dollars, of Eliza Armstrong, the thirteen-year-old daughter of a chimney sweep, in order to demonstrate how easy it was to procure young girls for prostitution. Stead then published an account of his investigations under the rather biblical title of "Maiden Tribute of Modern Babylon" and made it a *Pall Mall Gazette* extra. Although his motives were clearly benign and the purchase of the girl obviously an intrinsic part of the exposé, the editor, along with accomplices, was charged and briefly imprisoned for procurement. Even so, the storm of publicity he stirred up was instrumental in forcing a change in the law that same year, and the age of consent was raised from thirteen to sixteen. It was a remarkable demonstration of the power of the popular press. Stead had, in effect, turned a patrician publication into a tabloid that not only attracted many more readers with its human interest stories and accessible layout but also demonstrated that it was not afraid to take on the establishment. Like Stead himself, the *Pall Mall Gazette* of this period had the courage of its convictions.

Ironically, today's traders in child pornography and prostitution have little to fear from the hollow cries of moral outrage about pedophilia from the pragmatic descendants of the *Pall Mall Gazette*. Current tabloid editors, both British and American, know a sensational story when they smell one and have long since mastered the art of pandering to the worst instincts of a prurient readership while piously sermonizing in the margins. Few editors are willing to go to prison for practicing what they preach. Tabloid "debate," as a result, usually generates more heat than light and so helps to ensure that public discussion about child abuse is as overwrought as it is enlightened. Yet this is a relatively modern phenomenon. Contrast the pared-down press coverage of Florence Sally Horner's 1948 abduction and sexual abuse by Frank LaSalle (where little leaked into the papers at all until after her release, when the coverage was mainly brief, factual, and unsensational) with the firestorms of journalistic speculation about the 1996 JonBenet Ramsey murder.

Once, the boundary between factual reportage and titillating documentary-style fantasy was defined by the existence of publications like *Real Confessions*, *Real Romances*, and *Crime Confessions*; these were fact-derived entertainment. From the 1930s onward, *Crime Confessions* in particular specialized in turning spicy news stories into pulp fiction morality tales. Its editorial content could be said to comprise a mix of facts and "factoids" (the word "factoid" was coined by Norman Mailer in his 1973 Marilyn Monroe biography to denote a "fact" that does not actually exist before being reported in a magazine or newspaper) often reworked into stories that conformed to the principles of fiction rather than reportage. These magazines were Hillman Periodicals' response to Fawcett Publications' highly successful *True Confessions* title. If *True Confessions* mainly appealed to an audience of married women who enjoyed romantic syntheses of real-life stories, Hillman's titles sought to work the same trick with sometimes racier, crime-flavored source material and so cornered the market for this sort of "faction."

This is not to say that some mainstream newspapers were above the most lurid exaggeration in the holy cause of boosting circulation, but they rarely lapsed into dishing up the sort of the imaginative rehashes of the *Confessions*-type magazines. As for the mainstream newspaper journalists themselves, even the most rigorous were not always highly regarded. A few became distinguished novelists (for example, Ernest Hemingway and James M. Cain), and some of the more investigative types might occasionally acquire reputations involving something of the rough glamour of the private eye (an image much helped by movies such as *It Happened One Night* [1934] and *Foreign Correspondent* [1940]), but a staccato prose style and limited education marked them as the poor relations of belles lettres writing. Certainly the mannerisms, clichés, and canards of the 1940s press provide Humbert with great sport throughout *Lolita*. We may recall how he recasts and greatly enlivens a news report's dry factual reporting style in the case of G. Edward Grammar's uxoricide (see chapter 2) with his own fleshed-out version, and he also mocks errors in Ramsdale's local press report of his own wedding to Charlotte (one of Humbert's favorite poets, Rimbaud, comes out as Rainbow; today it would probably be Rambo).

Newspapers as artifacts turn up frequently throughout *Lolita*, fulfilling a variety of roles from fig leaf to memento mori. When Humbert masturbates with Lolita on his lap, he subsequently seeks to disguise his arousal with a newspaper. Waiting for Lolita's sleeping pill to take effect, he anxiously kills time in the various public spaces of the Enchanted Hunters Hotel and is by chance included in a flash photograph of a group of hotel wedding guests and so immortalized "insofar as the texture and print of small-town newspapers can be deemed immortal," he notes dryly in his memoir. Lolita's fascination with homely weddings as pictured by local newspaper photographers has already been noted. Newspapers also supply the diet of funnies that sustain Lolita on the protracted road trip, and, in one instance, a newspaper cartoon character unnerves Humbert (during an electrical storm, he either sees disguised Quilty or else hallucinates a malign caller wearing a grotesque Dick Tracy mask). On another occasion, while Humbert is having his hair ineptly cut by an elderly barber in the Midwest town of Kasbeam (and Lolita is having surreptitious sex with Quilty back at the motel), newspapers serve yet another purpose: yellowing news clippings produced by the sentimental barber to illustrate the exploits of his baseball-playing son belatedly reveal that the boy about whom he has been boasting has been dead for over thirty years. Humbert's delayed realization of this fact forms a melancholy mood counterpoint to the simultaneous sexual betrayal that neither he nor the readers can know about yet.

So much for the press's appearance in *Lolita*. Lolita's appearances in the press, from the Graham Greene/John Gordon spat onward, have usually been less than edifying.

Post-*Lolita*, the newspapers found they had a new shorthand label—and they could not have wished for a better one. "Lolita" was short, distinctive, easily pronounced, and rapidly acquired a meaning that was internationally understood—or rather misunderstood. Before long "Lolita," in the press sense, was a provocative teenage sex siren, a tart, a slut, a voracious and proactive seducer of middle-aged men. This Lolita was a factoid, a fabrication presented by the print media as a fact, thus acquiring a bogus new reality of its own. (Here it should be pointed out that Mailer's word, the invention of which was to come twenty years after *Lolita* was first published, would later become corrupted when CNN *Headline News* chose to use it as a diminutive, connoting a sort of minifact presented as an hors d'oeuvre to the more substantial news feast of the day. That meaning—etymologically unsound, since an -oid suffix usually means "resembling" or "like"—still occasionally surfaces in the media.)

Lolita's newfound notoriety did not depend exclusively on the printed media, but it was there that her newly resonant name continued to resonate. At the time of this writing, half a century since the first American publication of *Lolita*, the world's current number one female tennis star, at least as far as the press is concerned, is the California-based Russian Maria Yurievna Sharapova. No doubt Nabokov would have derived some enjoyment from the spectacle of a prodigiously talented expatriate Russian girl excelling at one of his favorite sports in his beloved adopted country, but he would also have groaned at the press epithets deemed suitable for someone whose only misdemeanor was to start out as a bratty-looking teenager: *the red-hot Russian . . . the Lolita of women's tennis . . .*

Lolita with a racket . . . and so on. Did Sharapova have a precursor? Indeed she did: fellow Russian Anna Kournikova was frequently dubbed the "Lobbing Lolita" in the press, but her retirement from competition—as well as her more conventional type of beauty—meant that journalists soon sought a successor and found her in the sometimes petulant young Sharapova, whose occasional teen sulkiness combined with her lithe physique made her an even better expression of the Lolita fantasy cliché. Those Lolita sobriquets are clearly meant to inject sex into the spectacle of a sweat-drenched young woman whose only visible desire has to do with winning a game of tennis.

The aggregation of power and significance in the press's Lolita code word has gradually grown over the years, but a single scandal was the rocket booster that put it into permanent orbit, and the *New York Post* was the launchpad.

In the early 1990s, the *Post* was between its two periods of ownership by Rupert Murdoch's News Corporation and languishing under the flagging ownership of soon-to-be-bankrupt Peter S. Kalikow. Not yet the out-and-out tabloid it would become, the *Post* was certainly not the only newspaper to take an interest in a tawdry Long Island saga of underage sex and near-fatal shooting. Through Amy Pagnazzo's column, however, it was the paper that assumed a kind of proprietorial and somewhat moralistic role about what it and every other paper dubbed the case of the Long Island Lolita. The prosaic lilt of that label with its four chiming Ls recalled the first two lines of a poem written some twenty years earlier by Anthony Burgess in celebration of Vladimir Nabokov's seventieth birthday.

> That nymphet's beauty lay less on her bones
> Than in her name's proclaimed two allophones.

Recalling the opening sentence of *Lolita* and suggesting that its heroine's life in the novel is inseparable from Humbert's obsession with everything about her—including the sound of her name—Burgess's lines also remind us that words were the medium that brought Lolita into the world. The more workmanlike vocabulary of newspaper headlines transmuted seventeen-year-old Amy Elizabeth Fisher into the Long Island Lolita and in doing so, in many people's eyes, placed the primary blame for a tangled and tawdry small-town scandal upon her. It may have been the right conclusion, but it was the wrong way to arrive at it.

The undisputed facts of the case, such as they can be objectively determined, are fairly well known and deserve only a brief recapitulation here. Amy Fisher, a sixteen-year-old student at Kennedy High School in Bellmore, Nassau County, began an affair with thirty-five-year-old married car mechanic Joseph Buttafuoco, then drifted into part-time prostitution, and ultimately shot Buttafuoco's wife Mary Jo in the head on her own doorstep. The long-running nature of the news story grew out of extended legal proceedings and the conflicting versions of events told by Fisher and Buttafuoco. Fisher, who disliked her disciplinarian father and was spoiled by her mother, depicted Buttafuoco as a willing lover whom she hoped would divorce his wife so he could marry her. Buttafuoco claimed never to have responded to Fisher's advances or to have had sex with her, let alone promise to leave his wife for her. Subsequent events made Buttafuoco's version sound highly suspect—he was jailed for the statutory rape of Fisher, then incurred a string of further convictions after moving to California. While legal proceedings were still going on, Fisher managed to damage her own case—with the help of *Hard Copy*, the syndicated tabloid news TV show that ran from 1989 to 1999—when in September 1992 she was covertly taped at a Massapequa gym talking to boyfriend Paul Makely about having sex in jail and the possible payoffs that notoriety would bring her. *Hard Copy* broadcast the tape, which hardly helped Fisher's credibility.

Journalist Amy Pagnazzo had covered the case for the *New York Post* under little illusion about Fisher's probable guilt but with much to say about the sexist attitudes that surrounded the case. "And now the term 'Lolita' is being applied to Amy Fisher, as if this alone would let grown men off the hook," quotes Amy Pagnazzo from her own column (or at least her character does in the only one of the three Amy Fisher TV movies with which Pagnazzo collaborated). "But while Amy may have been willing to have sex with an older married man in spirit, it does not make her willing under the law. It is by law statutory rape," Pagnazzo concludes. Tellingly, Pagnazzo, in her bid to play fair by Fisher, takes as a given the idea that the "Lolita" label carries with it a certain assumption of guilt. This particular TV movie, *The Amy Fisher Story*, features a plausible Drew Barrymore as the teenager from hell, while Pagnazzo is portrayed with an almost comical level of world-weary cynicism by Harley Jane Kozak, lip curling at every turn. She has one good line, worth quoting here because it contains a pleasing coincidence. After a police spokesman characterizes the shooting of Mary Jo Buttafuoco as the result of "a kind of fatal attraction thing," Pagnozzo/Kozak says, "Great—she's being accused of a movie." The movie in question (*Fatal Attraction*, 1987) had been directed by Adrian Lyne, the man who would spend most of the 1990s trying to get his movie of *Lolita* off the ground. Meanwhile, *The Amy Fisher Story* remains the best of a bad trio of TV movies, all of them essentially naive enactments of a tabloid story. This one at least does seek to represent both Fisher and Buttafuoco's versions in a single narrative.

Another TV movie, this time with Noelle Parker, was titled *Amy Fisher: My Own Story*, at least for its initial broadcast, but it soon acquired the punchier handle of *Lethal Lolita* in the budget video world for which it was always destined. Aware of the by now negative value-laden qualities of the Lolita name, Fisher naturally avoided sanctioning its use herself. Tame as well as one-sided, this TV movie represents Fisher's rebellious streak somewhat literally by putting a strawberry pink stripe in her hair. Noelle Parker looks much too nice to be the "monumental brat" (another of her ally Pagnazzo's characterizations) and cannot really suggest guile and meanness. Take one look at Drew Barrymore and you know she could be trouble, but Parker is undone by her own wholesomeness. A third TV movie contender, *Casualties of Love: The Long Island Lolita Story*, took the ill-advised route of representing Joseph Buttafuoco's version of the affair and is as dire in its execution as in its judgment. Jack Scalia plays Saint Joseph, and twenty-one-year-old Alyssa Milano embodies a slutty Amy.

Noelle Parker impersonates Amy Fisher in *Lethal Lolita*, one of the three TV movies inspired by the tawdry tabloid saga of Fisher and Joey Buttafuoco. (*Lethal Lolita*, I992, Infinity)

These TV movies are only interesting insofar as they are really visual versions of press accounts—all "factual" writing mixed with personal and biased opinions and played out like a crime show reenactment with a slightly bigger budget. The truth of the matter is that the Long Island Lolita case was a triumph of press labeling and marketing, and Lolita's name provided the sales hook. What actually transpired in Nassau County was a sad and shabby business that resulted in the serious wounding of a woman caught in the cross fire of two wildly dysfunctional people who were apparently incapable of communicating coherently with one another or anybody else. The saga's two principals would go on to demonstrate that malice and self-deception do not necessarily clear up with age. After serving a nine-year sentence for the shooting, Amy Fisher went on to become a writer, usually trading on her past notoriety while still seeming reluctant to take full responsibility for her own actions. "At the time, you know, it's very glorified in the tabloids and it became a big joke but you know what? It wasn't a joke," Fisher solemnly announced on CBS's *The Early Show* while promoting her latest book in 2003. "There was a woman gravely injured or could have been killed." Well, yes, it was Fisher herself who did the grave injuring, although her choice of words seems to distance herself from the event. Meanwhile, Joey Buttafuoco simply went on being Joey Buttafuoco, subsequently going to prison several times in connection with solicitation for prostitution, insurance fraud, and the illegal possession of ammunition. When Fisher finally decided to come face-to-face with him again for the edification of the TV audience of *Entertainment Tonight* in May 2006, the encounter soon became a Jerry Springer–type shouting match that sounded very much as if it might be picking up where a similar argument had left off in some motel room over a decade before. An older but clearly no wiser Buttafuoco sat stolidly in his chair, chin jutting truculently like Mussolini and spouting self-serving nonsense. Fisher

merely spat out pent-up resentment and walked off in tears. One
was reminded of Gore Vidal's observation about some disastrous
couple who were ideal for one another: the rocks in his head perfectly fit the holes in hers.

So the Long Island Lolita affair was far from being a classic crime
of passion—it was just a shabby scandal inflated by the tabloids.
Before it started, Lolita's name had already been compromised by
cumulative misunderstandings. By its conclusion, her image was,
in the minds of many newspaper readers, now inextricably linked
to that of charmless Amy Fisher.

Superficially similar cases surface from time to time, and the
tabloids welcome them warmly. In 1999, the British paper the *Sunday People* offered a sensationalized account of an English affair
whose main talking point was a teenage girl's successful bid to get
her father arrested for trying to prevent her from going out. However, it was what she was going out to do that preoccupied the *Sunday People*. The following extract from its report is something of a
classic example of the overheated genre.

> Shameful Truth about Wild Child Lolita, 15 Who Got Dad Locked
> Up; She STOLE a US Airman from His Wife; She LIED about
> Her Age to Snare Him; She's MAD for Sex with Servicemen; She
> JEERED at His Missus in Burger Bar.
>
> THE wild child who got her dad arrested when he tried to curb
> her antics is a marriage-breaking Lolita, *The Sunday People* can
> reveal.
>
> Georgina Brundle, 15, seduced American serviceman Peter Fos-
> ter, 25, after deliberately bumping into him at a roller-skating rink.

Another tabloid staple is represented by those intermittent cases
of male teachers running off with one of their female pupils. Here
it is virtually guaranteed that Lolita will be cited somewhere in the

tabloid press and beyond. Ex-teacher Gordon Sumner, a.k.a. rock star Sting, mentioned the teacher/schoolgirl cliché in his 1980 song "Don't Stand So Close to Me." It contains the line, "Just like the old man in that book by Nabokov." Ah the irony: if Lolita was too young, might vain Humbert not have winced at being dubbed an "old man" at thirty-six?

Less welcome in the tabloids are stories like that of Mark Blilie, a schoolteacher in Seattle who spent nearly four years in prison for having sex with a fifteen-year-old student, Toni Pala. The couple eventually married after Blilie's release from prison, and Pala consistently refused to assume the role convention would have her play. "I never felt like a victim," she said after their marriage. "I never felt that Mark was grooming me or preparing me." The tabloids have also notably neglected to give much space to the fact that Woody Allen's ten-year-plus marriage to Soon-Yi Previn has been thus far a stable and happy union.

Tabloid times were changing in other ways too. Lolita-tagged titillation tended to gravitate to cases like that of Georgina Brundle, while crimes involving pedophilia, kidnapping, and murder were often just too gruesome—or the victims too young—to risk implying that the little girls were somehow complicit in their own misfortune. Such cases were presented as horror stories rather than teenage temptress stories.

Along with the cases of ten-year-old Fusako Sano and teenager Tanya Kach mentioned in chapter 2, the top headline grabbers in this respect were Polly Klaas, Elizabeth Smart, and JonBenet Ramsey. Why, when some two thousand children go missing every year in the United States, do a handful of cases get all of the media attention? Well, Polly Hannah Klass was a twelve-year-old girl with an outgoing personality, an attractive kid from Petaluma, California, who was abducted in late 1993 and whose prankish life up to the point of her abduction played well in the press and on TV news reports. Her subsequent rape and murder played horribly, but there can be little doubt that the scenario of innocence defiled and destroyed had now acquired a media appeal of its own, so the Lolita tag was largely relegated to more flippant cases. Even so, there was hardly any featured instance of child rape, abduction, or murder in connection with which some pundit or psychologist would not invoke the name of Lolita.

In 2002, fourteen-year-old Elizabeth Smart was kidnapped from her bedroom by two homeless adherents of radical Mormon fundamentalism. Happily, she was found alive nine months later a few miles from her home in Salt Lake City. Less happily, she had been indoctrinated, imprisoned, rechristened, beaten, and raped by her captors and initially showed signs of Stockholm syndrome, that phenomenon whereby victims side with their oppressors, as newspaper heiress Patty Hearst had done when abducted by the self-styled Symbionese Liberation Army terrorist group. At least Smart survived. Both she and Klaas were attractive white girls from a middle-class background. The majority of missing children are not, and as far as the tabloids were concerned, there were now two crude stereotype options for deciding which cases to spotlight: complicit tramp or angelic victim. In both cases, looks were all-important, and with around two thousand cases a year to choose from, the papers usually had several photogenic candidates to select from when deciding which case to focus upon. Even so, one particularly grotesque case would blur even those crass distinctions.

Six-year-old JonBenet Ramsey was way too young to be a Lolita in the press sense, but this did not stop her mother making a grotesque bid to sexualize her anyway by means of the now-familiar beauty pageant makeup and outfits that the world at large would only see after the child was murdered in bizarre and unclear circumstances. Kids like JonBenet were traditionally only celebrities in the melancholy world of tiny-tot beauty pageants where, painted and powdered, they would ape the sexual mannerisms of female adults, unaware that part of the future they were invoking might, with very bad luck, become part of their present. In a CNN discussion broadcast when the Elizabeth Smart case first came to public attention, writer James Wolcott of *Vanity Fair* magazine said, tellingly: "When I saw that Fox's coverage was titled 'Where Is Elizabeth Smart?' my thought was well, you know, who killed Laura Palmer? It's like *Twin Peaks* in that you have sort of a blonde vision of innocence, of maidenhood . . . it plays into the JonBenet story. Jon Benet was, you know, this sort of Lolita-ish beauty pageant contestant and what makes it even more sort of archetypal is that Elizabeth Smart played the harp. You can't get more angelic than that."

The changing face of scandal. In the late 1940s the two-year-long abduction of young Sally Horner by Frank LaSalle attracted only skimpy local press coverage in the United States. The 2006 release of kidnapped Natascha Kampusch in Austria, by contrast, generated an international media feeding frenzy. (LaSalle and Horner picture, 1950, *Lima News*, Lima, Ohio; Natascha Kampusch magazine cover, 2006, *News*, Verlagsgruppe NEWS Gesellschaft m.b.H., Austria)

Perhaps you can. The world at large was startled by the press photos and TV footage of Natascha Kampusch, the ten-year-old Austrian girl abducted for eight years whose story was outlined in chapter 2. Suddenly free at eighteen, she truly looked like a saint, her gaze clear and her face calmly beautiful even if her fingers were twitchy claws when she sat for press and TV interviews. The overall press treatment of that extraordinary affair brought the press's Lolita fixation to what may yet prove to have been some sort of plateau, if not a conclusion. An article by Stefanie Marsh in *The Australian* magazine (motto: Keeping the Nation Informed) contained the following Humbertian information: "It is thought that Priklopil (Kampusch's abductor) came to be dominated by his Lolita. He may have viewed it as the flowering of a genuine relationship. Or perhaps the sight of a fully developed woman, even one modelled to his specifications, increasingly left him cold." Except that Humbert only *thought* Lolita would grow unappealing to him; she never did.

There will, sooner or later, be a movie of the Kampusch affair and that, along with the brilliantly stage-managed TV interview that was granted and syndicated worldwide, perhaps suggests that in the future the tabloids will no longer be the chief media source of titillating reportage in such cases. The ever greater freedoms enjoyed by movies, the Internet, and cable TV will perhaps make these the natural media to explore and exploit the news aspects of such relationships. Gone are the days when tame TV movies like *Lethal Lolita* cannot include the scandalous details; HBO and the Internet can show pretty much anything. Whatever dramatic forms the Natascha Kampusch saga eventually takes, it will of course have her book to draw upon: Kampusch is turning her experience—and the notes she made in captivity—into what will surely be a bestseller. While imprisoned, she herself read a lot of books (a literate Lolita, this) including *Alice's Adventures in*

Wonderland and *Robinson Crusoe*. Perhaps Kampusch, with help and good fortune, will return her own child abuse/love story to the medium in which Nabokov cast his. One commentator, Rainer Just, suggests that Kampusch's story has already been written by others. In an article for the Austrian literary magazine *Wespennest* he wrote, "Perhaps it ought to be written in the tradition of Vladimir Nabokov, as a deconstructive Lolita of the twenty-first century: Na-ta-scha—the tip of the tongue taking a trip of three steps . . . or perhaps written as a film from the very start, as an imaginary spool of haunting pictures . . . because the medium of film offers the perfect opportunity to convey the complex psycho-logic of an infinite desire."

That final assertion might elicit a particularly hollow laugh from a man who spent seven years setting up his movie of *Lolita* and then almost as many more trying to get it shown. He was Adrian Lyne, an English film director with a combative Irish streak, who had set his heart on doing *Lolita* justice on the screen. The tabloids pilloried him at every turn, frequently echoing John Gordon's spluttering outrage in the *Sunday Express* of 1955. It might even be argued that they had indirectly helped set him up to fail through their contribution to the mood of child abuse hysteria that immediately preceded his first attempts to put the movie together. In 1983, the McMartin Pre-School affair seemed, by its bizarre nature, to defy even the most dedicated tabloid attempts to cheapen the proceedings. Some of them, however, were up to the challenge. The McMartin Pre-School was located in Manhattan Beach, California, and there, it was alleged by the mother of one of the attending children, her son had been sexually abused by staff and others. On top of this accusation, there soon came surreal allegations about staff traveling to zoos in search of sexual encounters with giraffes, about orgies in car washes, tales of underground tunnels, and alleged sightings of airborne witches.

Literally hundreds of allegations of abuse followed, many of which were supported by the equally fantastic findings of a Los Angeles abuse therapy outfit called the Children's Institute International, which concluded that well over three hundred children had been abused in this satanic corner of Manhattan Beach. That it arrived at these conclusions only after asking highly leading questions of the preschoolers should have alerted everyone, but the media had a field day, and the story monopolized TV and print media in California and beyond. A reporter for the KABC television station, Wayne Satz, broadcast very biased reports that seemed to accept the parents' side of things unquestioningly—and then had an affair with an employee of the Children's Institute International who had conducted some of the institute's interviews with the children. The grim farce dragged on for six years, necessitating two hugely expensive trials that concluded, in 1990, with all charges being dropped.

The firestorm of public outrage that press and TV had kept stoking demanded a conclusion, however. Since the whole business was clearly a farrago fueled by the imaginations of children who had been browbeaten by suggestible parents, the only verity upon which everyone could agree was that child abuse was a very bad thing and demanded extreme reactions, even when nothing had happened. This, of course, is the unwelcome outcome when real life fails to conform to the easy characterizations of pulp fiction or tabloid simplification.

At the start of the 1990s, therefore, Adrian Lyne's nascent movie project began with the severe handicap of being pitched in a public atmosphere far more febrile than any that had existed when timorous Kubrick tiptoed around *Lolita*. Thinking was out, hysteria was in, and no amount of serious artistic intent was going to cut much ice. Even the sporadically rumored contributions of distinguished litterateurs such as Harold Pinter, Tom Stoppard, and David Mamet merely fueled the tabloid suspicion that art was once again going to be used as a highbrow excuse for smut. Nothing much changes. Lyne, however, was relentless in his efforts to bring Nabokov's tale of infinite desire to the screen in a way that would, after Kubrick's patchy misfire, do it some sort of justice. He pressed on.

[II]

TAKE TWO:
Once More, with Feeling

ADRIAN LYNE BATTLED HEROICALLY TO GET HIS FILM OF *LOLITA*
off the ground. The climate of public opinion toward any debate
about pedophilia was now deeply hostile, far more so than in the
1970s or 1980s, let alone the early 1960s. This was bad enough, but
it was not all. Lyne's first (and some would say his biggest) obstacle
to making a distinguished movie of one of the twentieth century's
greatest and most allusive novels was his own track record.

Born in 1941 in Peterborough, England, Lyne had learned how
to make films by directing TV commercials during what was London's golden period of advertising during the 1970s. In that decade,
London's advertising kudos eclipsed even that of Madison Avenue,
and ambitious young creatives from all over the world flocked to the
British capital to experience the highly inventive buzz of the major
agencies' offices. Like his English contemporaries Alan Parker and
Ridley Scott, Adrian Lyne had seen the TV commercial—which
often had a bigger minute-by-minute budget than most feature

films—as a springboard for a Hollywood movie career. It was a real-
istic ambition and it was achieved by all three of them. Alan Parker
became a protean film director whose only discernible style was
that he had no style at all; *Bugsy Malone, Midnight Express, Fame,*
and *Angel Heart* have little in common with one another either in
terms of subject matter or visual style, but all were successful. Ridley Scott had also worked as a production designer and TV director
before moving into commercials, and his early movies, including
Alien, Blade Runner, and *Legend,* all display a powerful visual style
and a strong sense of cinematic energy.

By contrast, looking at Adrian Lyne's movies up to the early
1990s it is hard to see anything more than a talented and slick professional at work. His first Hollywood picture was *Foxes* (1980),
a routine movie about the excesses of youth in the San Fernando
Valley—sex, drugs, and ex-Coppertone kid Jodie Foster. Next came
Flashdance (1984), an urban fairy tale about a dancing welder from
Pittsburgh (Jennifer Beals) who Has a Dream. It was a hit and was
followed by a trio of even more successful but rather shallow erotic
movies: *Nine 1/2 Weeks* (1986), *Fatal Attraction* (1987), and *Indecent
Proposal* (1993). Admittedly *Jacob's Ladder* (1990) was in there too,
and that was a very well-handled post-Vietnam psychological tour
de force that in some ways foreshadowed M. Night Shyamalan's hit
of 1999, *The Sixth Sense.* Otherwise Lyne's movie career seemed to
be dogged by his roots in advertising—plenty of style but little substance. Also, some of his films seemed, perhaps by coincidence, to
hang on the coattails of the slightly younger Alan Parker's more
prolific output. After all, Parker's *Fame* had preceded Lyne's *Dirty
Dancing,* Parker's *Birdy* had anticipated *Jacob's Ladder,* and even
budding star Jodie Foster had graced Parker's kids-as-gangsters
pastiche *Bugsy Malone* (1976) four years before *Foxes* was made.

Lyne therefore started the long haul to set up *Lolita* with the distinct advantage of some box office hits under his belt but with the

burden of a mixed critical reputation and a popular reputation for directing glossy mainstream erotica. Some critics might acknowledge his visual flair and his commercial instincts, but no one spoke of Adrian Lyne as an auteur, a status that even Stanley Kubrick had by now attained.

Lyne always bitterly resented the advertising tag, maintaining that he had only ever seen commercials as an opportunity to learn filmmaking skills, and he was also resentful about his reputation as a crowd-pleaser (he had, though, no qualms about reshooting the end of *Fatal Attraction* in response to audience opinion poll findings). Approaching his fiftieth birthday, Lyne was therefore understandably inclined to take on the formidable challenge of *Lolita*, a literary work of art he had long adored and that was finally optioned to him in 1990, prior to the shooting of *Indecent Proposal*. It was to prove a case of excruciatingly bad timing.

At this time, the protracted McMartin Pre-School affair was reaching the end of its second and final trial, and Amy Fisher would soon make her first fateful visit to Joseph Buttafuoco's car repair shop in Long Island, ensuring that Lolita's name would stay in the headlines for years for all the wrong reasons.

Lyne's *Lolita* project advanced very slowly, even by the glacial standards that prevail in what is known in the trade as Movie Development Hell. Since pedophilia was now a harder sell than ever in Hollywood, few were interested. The independent U.S. production company Carolco Pictures, Inc. expressed interest in bankrolling the project, however. Carolco had enjoyed great success with the Rambo movies and *Terminator 2* and also produced Alan Parker's *Angel Heart* and Sir Richard Attenborough's *Chaplin*. Lyne now wrote a thirty-five-page outline titled "Preparatory Notes on Nabokov's Novel." In it he immediately identified what looked like an intractable problem: how do you make the audience care about an incarnation of Humbert? Robbed of the ruined grandeur

he occasionally achieves as an invisible narrator in a book, a corpo-
real Humbert becomes what? A villain? A fall guy? A lovable rogue?
An antihero? A monster? A moral leper? Would a movie audience
have any sympathy with him at all? How would it play in Peoria? In
his treatment, Lyne considered starting the movie with Humbert
in prison.

"If the audience understands that Humbert is paying his dues, it
may help our case," Lyne wrote, proposing a device that, ironically
enough, recalled the mechanical prescriptive morality of the Hays
Code. Lyne's completed treatment went to a succession of writers,
each charged with solving the primary dilemma of making Humbert a lead character with whom the audience might somehow identify, as well as tackling a daunting number of other structural and
stylistic problems posed by this allegedly unfilmable novel. ("You
can have the movie rights," the otherwise uncooperative Maurice
Girodias had once said to Vladimir Nabokov. "They'll never make
a movie of that.")

James Dearden, the writer of *Fatal Attraction*, was the first to be
commissioned, but his script, set in the present day, was rejected.
The British playwright Harold Pinter was then recruited. This might
have turned out well, since even those of us who find Pinter's reputation as a great playwright baffling can still find much to admire in
his movie adaptations. Pinter had made a creditable screenwriting
job of everything from *The Last Tycoon* and *The French Lieutenant's
Woman* to *The Quiller Memorandum* and *The Handmaid's Tale*, so
he might perhaps do *Lolita* proud. Unfortunately, Pinter was always
virulently anti-American in his politics as well as socially subver-
sive in his film adaptations, at least whenever he could get away with
it. One suspects he did not much care for Nabokov anyway. Was
Pinter, after all, the best man to render the greatest novel of an apo-
litical, pro-America, nonsatirical writer for the screen? The answer
came early on when Pinter's submitted screenplay began with the

words, "My name is Humbert, you won't like me . . . don't come any further with me if you believe in moral values." The script was shown to various studios and distributors, but the consensus was that it was chilly and distant and would need an actor of impossibly rakish charm to imbue Humbert with humanity. Charm was not really what was required, and even the proposed casting of Hugh Grant as a lightweight and too-young Humbert (a serious suggestion at one point) was not going to salvage an icy script characterization. Harold Pinter was out. Rumors that Tom Stoppard might be involved remained nothing more than rumors.

By late 1994, an increasingly desperate Adrian Lyne heeded Hollywood producer Richard Zanuck's suggestion to read some forty pages of a script written by a New York journalist, Stephen Schiff, years earlier. In 1990, at his agent's request, Schiff had taken a speculative stab at writing a screenplay (his first ever) for *Lolita*. Since Schiff's agent was Richard Zanuck's wife, Lili, this was hardly a shot in the dark, but Schiff had abandoned the project after about forty pages when America's moral climate seemed to render any proposed movie of *Lolita* unfeasible. Now, almost four years on, there was a meeting between Lyne, Schiff, and Zanuck at Zanuck's Beverly Hills office. Schiff too was asked if he could set the film in the present day, an absurd idea that he sensibly rebuffed, arguing that Lolita's story was inseparable from the context of its time.

"Nabokov set his novel in 1947," Schiff later wrote, "a singular moment in American cultural history—years before the finny, funny Fifties; before the invention of the great American teenager and the distinct consumer culture that sprang up to serve it." A pointless ten-year time lag had helped to rob Kubrick's film of any authentic context, and a forty-year dislocation would surely have rendered *Lolita*'s plot, as written by Nabokov, entirely meaningless. The Beverly Hills meeting was amiable, but Schiff simply had no track record in movies. Despite this, more in hope than expectation, he went home and returned to the task of writing a script for *Lolita* with renewed vigor. Richard Zanuck was still the film's putative producer at this stage, and he and Lyne next hedged their bets by commissioning David Mamet as the big-name writer who might finally deliver the goods, as well as bring extra cultural cachet to the enterprise.

Mamet promised to be an even more fascinating choice than Pinter. Quite apart from his screenplays for others, by this time the playwright had already directed four films himself: *House of Games, Things Change, Homicide,* and *Oleanna.* His grasp of the movie medium was proven (even if his film of his own play *Oleanna* captured little of the power of any of the major stage versions), and his early 1990s tally of some twenty well-received plays had made him world famous. Mamet's main strengths, though, appeared to lie in depicting men at work or play in abrasive urban situations; only *Oleanna*—a two-hander featuring a university professor accused of sexual harassment by a female student—seemed to hint at any thematic connection with *Lolita.* In the end, Mamet's script, like Pinter's, would leave Lyne and Zanuck dissatisfied, at which point they turned back, perhaps desperately, to Stephen Schiff. He sent them his newly completed script and they gave him the job. The novice who had never written a screenplay before had seen off Dearden, Pinter, and Mamet.

— — —

Dominique Swain was another novice. Born in Malibu, California, in 1980, the same year Adrian Lyne made his Hollywood debut with *Foxes,* she had little acting experience before getting the part of Lolita. She had failed an audition for Neil Jordan's *Interview with the Vampire* (Kirsten Dunst eventually won the part of Claudia) and made a brief uncredited appearance in a film written by Ian Mc-

Ewan and directed by Joseph Rubin, *The Good Son* (1993). Sporty, outgoing, artistic, and a straight-A high school student, Swain at fourteen was an interesting-looking girl rather than a conventionally pretty one. She was clearly intelligent and seemingly undaunted by the audition process. In a riveting videotape of her audition for the part of Lolita, with Jeremy Irons playing Humbert, she is no showbiz show-off kid but still comes over as precociously witty and self-assured. At one point she mimics Lyne's English accent, which, she suggests, is so much more sinister than an American one for delivering a line like "You murdered my mother." If Swain's physical development could have been arrested at the time of that audition, she would have been even better than she eventually was in the movie. But by the time they started shooting she was already looking older and more strapping and can actually be seen to be growing up during the film . . . albeit out of sequence due to the dislocated nature of shooting schedules. It hardly matters. After beating a reported twenty-five hundred applicants to the part, Swain turned out to be the film's undisputed success story. She would be a wonderful Lolita: rude, loud, childlike, touching, dreamy, goofy, cruel, sad, feisty, sexy, and funny. She would do it by channeling her own personality into the part and in this was expertly guided by Adrian Lyne, the father of two daughters. Dominique Swain actually seemed to thrive on a lack of acting experience. Not knowing how to do it right can, with careful guidance and good luck, sometimes have the benign opposite effect too—not knowing how to do it wrong. Journalist Stephen Schiff was already proof of this, having turned in the excellent script Lyne needed.

Schiff's script is the crucial backbone of the film. In his introduction to its published version he wrote, "Most among our company actually looked upon the Kubrick version as a kind of 'what not to do.'" Schiff, however, did not choose to view that film again, although he had a vaguely benign recollection of it. Instead, he returned to the source. As well as respecting the shape of the novel (Schiff understood that you simply cannot lose the scene-setting Annabel Leigh episode or the one-year road trip), he also included a wealth of fine detail, most of it inessential to the plot but happily standing in for the subtle texture of a book filled with illusions and allusions. For example, Schiff seems fascinated with the artifacts and products of Lolita's world, the minutiae that occasionally divert Humbert but really exist outside of his orbit.

"I began thinking about the uniquely twisted and passionate relationships American girls often have with food," Schiff reflected. Some of the resultant bits of business along these lines were cut from the final film but some remain. For example, Humbert brings bananas to Lolita in the motel cabin where she deceives him with Quilty (here Swain introduces her English/American accent observation again, mimicking Jeremy Irons's pronunciation of bananas with its long middle "a"). A banana features again in a car scene where Lolita inserts the peeled fruit into her mouth and then absent-mindedly withdraws it again, unbitten but now with long twin furrows scored by her front teeth. Also in the car there is a playful scene with a jawbreaker where un-American Humbert eventually wrests the sticky globe from her mouth with his fingers after inquiring what it is ("It's a jawbreaker. It's supposed to break your jaw. Want one?"). A scene that was cut involved Lolita "educating" Humbert about the mystique of the Oreo cookie and the correct technique for eating one ("She breaks it in half, and slides the cream-covered side through her teeth until the cream is devoured"). None of this, apart from the first example where in the book Humbert says he bought a bunch of bananas for his monkey, is Nabokov's, but all of it perfectly matches the novel's delight in patterns of repetitive detail and observed behavior and helps to give the flesh-and-blood Dolores Haze specific tastes and a "real" self-sufficient personality, something she was denied when seen solely through Humbert's eyes.

Humbert's eyes, no longer the distorting lenses through which everything is seen, now have to be shown on-screen, along with the rest of him. This was the fundamental, perhaps irresolvable problem of *Lolita*—this and finding an actor possessing both the skill and the nerve to play him. Unknown fourteen-year-old actresses have no established career to compromise, but middle-aged actors do. Jeremy Irons, being a well-respected if not exactly beloved actor in his homeland of Britain, first balked at the risk (and this despite Harold Pinter's sweeping recommendation: "If you want an actor who isn't afraid to look bad, get Jeremy Irons"). Irons was eventually talked into it, perhaps because of his belief that his ultimate professional guiding principle should be "not to be embarrassed at my retrospective." He was certainly an outspoken and intelligent champion of the project throughout, although, unlike what had confronted James Mason, Irons's personal challenge was immense: he had to perform in several sexually charged scenes with a fourteen-year-old girl who was constantly being attended on set by her mother, a tutor, and a body double. Outside, the tabloid hounds were already baying. In the audition videotape with Swain (a violent argument is one of the scenes they rehearse), Irons manages to be kind and solicitous with her between exchanging violent and aggressive in-character insults. It set the ambiguous tone for the project. No matter what the level of professionalism, an uneasy personal chemistry would ensue because it is hard for a forty-eight-year-old man to play out violent arguments and sexual shenanigans with a high school girl. This movie would not be an easy one for leading man or director, but Lyne doggedly persisted, casting Irons and then looking for suitable supporting actors.

Melanie Griffith, a tinny-voiced actress not without her detractors, was cast as Charlotte Haze. This news was seen as another unpromising signal by many movie fans who were also admirers of the book, who were hoping for the best while fearing the worst.

More positively Frank Langella, a fine and imposing actor, was cast as Quilty. Richard Zanuck left the project before shooting began and the producer's role was taken over by Mario Kassar of Carolco and Joel B. Michaels. In 1994, shooting finally got under way. The main locations were in California, Louisiana, New Mexico, North Carolina, and Texas. Everyone in the crew was walking on egg-shells, partly out of consideration for the well-publicized presence of their fourteen/fifteen-year-old leading lady (she turned fifteen on August 12, 1995) and partly because of the hostility that already sur-rounded their controversial project in Hollywood and beyond. On location in the South, Lyne said he frequently half expected some redneck sheriff to burst in at any moment to close down the pro-ceedings before the movie was even shot. As for sexual impropriety, all due care was taken, some of it risible. When Swain sat on Irons's lap, a cushion or board was placed between them. When it was nec-essary for Lolita to run a hand up Humbert's thigh or vice versa, the body double took over. The weather, doing what weather does, delayed things. Melanie Griffith fell sick. The original cinematogra-pher had to be replaced after shooting began. Jeremy Irons had real problems with some of the sex scenes. And the only person to sail through the experience with any degree of equanimity was Domi-nique Swain. Happy to be the center of attention and untroubled by the one aspect of things that troubled everybody else, she burst into tears only when Irons snapped at her for ill-advisedly telling him what to do. The director occasionally had to keep her in line when her exuberant behavior went beyond animating Lolita and threatened to disrupt the shoot. His original instincts about her had been right, though: whatever happened to the movie, it looked like it would at least have a terrific Lolita. They wrapped in late 1995. They started editing in 1996. Then the real battles began.

Carolco Pictures, Inc., the once successful independent com-pany that was bankrolling the film, suddenly fell upon hard times, the result of general decline and two particularly expensive flops, *Cutthroat Island* and *Show Girls*. As bankruptcy loomed, Carolco sold *Lolita* to a big French corporation, Chargeurs, that had already acquired the movie production and distribution company Pathé back in 1992. Now, in 1996, Chargeurs was demerging Pathé, an outfit for which, it was assumed, *Lolita* would be an ideal property. After the deal was done, Pathé's optimism soon turned to concern (and Lyne's hope to despair) when a new law, the Child Pornography Prevention Act of 1996, was enacted in the United States. Aimed at Internet pornographers who used computer graphics to simulate images of children having sex (even when no real children were involved), it threw up a potential killer obstacle to distributing the new *Lolita* at all in the United States. The reason was that the act proscribed any visual depiction that was "or appeared to be" a child having explicit sex. This scattergun definition, although perhaps worthy in original intention, had huge potential ramifications for a wide range of mainstream media. An act that would retrospectively ban Volker Schlöndorff's *The Tin Drum* (1979) outright or remove the Claire Danes/Leonardo DiCaprio bedroom scene from *Romeo + Juliet* (1996) looked likely to be challenged in the courts, but no one was eager to be the first challenger. Pathé nervously assembled lawyers to see what their acquisition might be up against in the crucial American market. One particular lawyer was nominated to go through the film with a fine-tooth comb to ensure that it did not become the first test case to challenge the Child Pornography Prevention Act of 1996.

Lyne and Schiff battled with that lawyer (a pornography specialist whose most famous client, Schiff alleges, had been underage porn actress Traci Lords), and after the usual horse trading found that one of the few remaining areas of dispute was what they called the Comics Scene. This referred to the film's treatment of something mentioned in chapter 5 where naked Humbert would, he tells us, on hot afternoons, sit in a motel cabin armchair with Lolita sitting on his lap reading the funnies. It was to form one of the film's quintessential scenes, fixing perfectly Lolita's simultaneous habitation of the realms of childhood and adulthood, and it managed to achieve this mainly because Schiff and Lyne had upped the ante. In a hot and shadowy motel room penetrated by three shafts of sunlight, beneath a dust-caked ceiling fan and its depending spiral of well-used flypaper, Lolita sits on reclining Humbert's lap dreamily perusing the comic strip adventures of Invisible Scarlet O'Neil and Brenda Breeze. A fly lands on the newspaper and is brushed away. She is wearing the top half of a pair of pajamas, he is wearing the bottom half (a device, incidentally, used more innocently in the publicity shots for *The Pajama Game* [1957] featuring Doris Day and John Raitt). Initially both are motionless and Lolita's look of calm pleasure seems to be prompted by nothing more than her languorous enjoyment of the funnies; but as she braces her foot against the floor and they begin to rock gently back and forth, it is clear that they are having protracted, almost soporific sex. It is a genuinely erotic scene enhanced by the audience's delayed realization and all the more disturbing because here for once Lolita is shown as apparently complicit—contented even. Some rather more explicit shots were removed, including one of a fly landing on Lolita's bare midriff and crawling northward), but the scene remains powerful—simultaneously very disturbing and visually rather beautiful, a calculated paradox that perfectly encapsulates the fundamental appeal of the novel. Unfortunately, it also encapsulated why people were afraid of it. The scene survived more or less intact in spirit. As yet, U.S. distribution for *Lolita* was still unsecured.

"Had we released Lolita in the '70s or '80s," Schiff said, "I believe it would have easily made its way into distribution. But the culture has contracted since then. And even if it hasn't, its gatekeepers believe it has."

Distribution would prove a nightmare and was not helped by Pathé's growing timidity in the face of possible scandal and bad reviews. In early 1997, less than three months after JonBenet Ramsey had been found dead in her parents' subbasement, no one wanted to distribute *Lolita* in the United States. Adrian Lyne received many highly complimentary comments from the studios, but none of them would distribute it in the prevailing atmosphere. "It's a really good movie," one studio head told the *Washington Post* on condition of anonymity. "But it's not something we're going to pick up."

Lyne claimed to have received twenty or thirty letters from agents and executives saying how overwhelmed they were by the film. "They tell me 'it's your best work.' And suddenly they've become mute." One by one the American studios said no.

In a strange echo of what happened to Nabokov's novel back in the 1950s, Pathé effectively gave up on distributing it in the United States at all and looked to Europe. They perhaps hoped that a critical success there might kick-start its prospects on this side of the Atlantic. This seemed unlikely, despite the recent precedent of John Dahl's *The Last Seduction* (1994), a cable TV movie that was shown on HBO and forgotten until it wowed European audiences in theaters, subsequently earning a U.S. theatrical release and rumors of a thwarted Academy Award nomination for star Linda Fiorentino (not permitted because the movie had premiered on TV) and becoming a neo-noir classic.

Adrian Lyne's *Lolita* eventually premiered in Spain, at the 1997 San Sebastian Film Festival. It received mixed reviews and subsequently fared poorly in Spain. Italy loved it. In Germany it stirred up many public protests and was subsequently hard to see in that country. In Britain it received a certificate with no trouble whatsoever, something that stirred up tabloid outrage (Jeremy Irons was reported as saying he would leave the country if it were banned). A few U.S. critics became "Lolita Tourists," pursuing European screenings in order to form an opinion. *Variety* was not alone in taking the doctrinaire view that *Lolita*, like any Adrian Lyne film, necessarily amounted to little more than a succession of skillful art direction flourishes. Generally, though, the critics were impressed if a little surprised by the quantum leap in quality that Lyne had demonstrated.

"[He] has translated Nabokov's classic with sensitivity, intelligence and style," wrote Jack Kroll in *Newsweek*. Caryn James called Lyne's *Lolita* "an eloquent tragedy laced with wit and a serious, disturbing work of art" in the *New York Times* Sunday Arts & Leisure section. The British trade journal *Screen International* said, "The US distributors who have refused to touch this story of illicit paternal passion have a lot to answer for . . . [it] manages to be at once glossily watchable, psychologically complex, and morally mature. . . . *Lolita* is (Lyne's) best yet—by quite a wide margin."

In the end, the cable network *Showtime* bought the U.S. rights to the movie and broadcast it to any American household that subscribed to their channel in the summer of 1998. Despite limited screenings in New York, Los Angeles, and a few other cities, the movie—forty years after the novel was freely published—was to all intents and purposes banned from theatrical release in the United States, not by the censor but by the movie industry itself.

I first saw Adrian Lyne's *Lolita* in 1998 at a sparsely attended afternoon performance in a Warner Village cineplex in London's Leicester Square. There were no riots. The film can now be acquired on DVD in the United States and most other territories. To say that tracking it down is worth the effort would damn with faint praise a superior film that is not only far more faithful to Nabokov's novel than the 1962 version but more faithful to the novel than any film version might reasonably have been expected to be. Admittedly its early Riviera sequence, that crucial Annabel Leigh episode, reinforces the worries of those who dislike Lyne's fondness for soft-focus photography and pretty compositions, but that seems to be a second-unit aberration. Also, Jeremy Irons's Humbert comes over throughout, in the actor's own words, as "a rather weak and misguided man," so those hoping for a roaring, ruined grotesque will not find it in his emotional yet apologetic and socially inept Humbert. Melanie Griffith's performance as Charlotte is underpowered but brief; her delivery of some lines sounds as if she is reading them out loud for the first time. Otherwise this *Lolita* positively overflows with good things. Schiff knew that for most of the story Quilty should be an evil shadow, not an extroverted scene-stealer, and wrote the part accordingly. When Quilty finally emerges into the light from his succession of chiaroscuro lairs, Frank Langella embodies him quite magnificently, giving a full-blooded (in every sense) portrayal of Nabokov's unhinged villain at bay. Perhaps Langella should have played Humbert instead—or as well.

Many minor pleasures reside in the film's evocative locations, the almost fanatical attention to period detail (even the napkins and glass covers at the Enchanted Hunters Hotel bear a beautifully realized period logo), the inclusion of authentic popular songs from 1947 and 1948, exquisite sets, and beautiful cinematography. And the script of great literacy and imagination commendably blurs the line between dialog adapted from the novel and lines newly written. Most of the neologisms are of course Schiff's, but he freely admits to retaining one or two of Pinter's trademark squibs from the earlier script. For example: "You look one hundred percent better when I can't see you," says fractious passenger Lolita to exasperated driver Humbert at one point. Meanwhile, Humbert's deadpan verdict on Charlotte's salad—"perfectly judged"—is both Pinter and Pinter-esque, one of those phrases that is somehow unsettling because of its awkward application.

Some things are artfully reinvented: for example, Lolita's summer camp (cryptic Camp Q in the book) becomes Camp Kewattomie,

which can still be abbreviated to Camp Kew to chime with Clare
Quilty's nickname Cue, although the rhyme is never actually
deployed in the film. Certain tiny details from the book are also
included, perhaps as miniature examples of Ars Gratia Artis: in an
unfamiliar hotel room Lolita mistakes a closet door for that of the
bathroom and laughs embarrassedly as she backs out and closes it
again; in a tiny gesture as she enters a store, she unself-consciously
tweaks her skirt loose from the cleft in her buttocks after leaving the
car she has been sitting in for hours. Nabokov wrote both vignettes
and dozens more like them, and Schiff's faithful but hardly nec-
essary retention of some of them seems like a conspiratorial nod
toward those rereaders of the novel who remember everything. He
even adds a very Nabokovian touch that does not come from the
book. When thirteen-year-old Humbert is preparing (alas, in vain)
to possess Annabel in the long-lost world of the 1920s Riviera, he
takes as a souvenir a bit of ribbon trim from the *broderie anglaise*
of her long underpants. How many members of the movie audience recognize that ribbon when it reappears, unannounced, as a
bookmark in middle-aged Humbert's diary in Ramsdale? Perhaps
as many as the number of readers who identify some of of Humbert's more arcane literary references in the novel. Everyone does
not need to get the more obscure allusions, but it is nice if those
references make artistic sense when they are spotted.

The film score and the featured music are particularly successful. Ennio Morricone's score underpins the film's shifting moods
hauntingly, particularly in Humbert's last desolate hours of freedom. Lolita's enthusiastic if tuneless sing-along participation with
contemporary novelty records on the radio—songs such as Louis
Prima's "Civilization," Jack McVea's "Open the Door, Richard," and,
perhaps most memorably, "Tim-Tay-Shun" (Jo Stafford's redneck
reworking of "Temptation")—seem somehow even more fitting than
the jukebox hits of mainstream crooners hinted at in the book.

In terms of exteriors, some decisions are inspired: a TeePee Motel (pastiche conical cabins) was a genuine disused and overgrown novelty motel that the filmmakers came across by accident, tidied up, and used because its compellingly tacky appeal summed up several of the more fragmented examples of commercial hospitality kitsch featured in the novel. The heartbreakingly plausible house in Coalmont where Humbert eventually finds Dolores and Richard Schiller living in poverty is a triumphant invention and fabrication, purposely built for the scene. The towns of Luckenback, El Paso, San Antonio, Wharton, Richmond, and Lake Buchanan all suggest hazy color variants of monochrome Archer, the paradigmatic vanishing Texan town featured in Peter Bogdanovich's *The Last Picture Show*. An early scene where Humbert goes to collect Lolita from summer camp features a quite lovely tableau with sun streaming through a glade that looks like Humbertian heaven, an Arcadia fully populated with young Camp Kewattomie girls happily waving and smiling in a kitsch/erotic tableau that sets his most elusive fantasy in a romantic Post-impressionist landscape ("[I] had visually possessed dappled nymphets in parks," writes Humbert of those frustrated European days prior to his arrival in the land of plenty).

Then there are the precisely observed details of motel cabins, general stores, garages, schools, and the sudden unexpectedly vast swathes of contrasting wasteland and highway, lush woods and quiet towns, an oppressive barber shop, sudden sparky interludes like an electric storm with its mighty cracks, and a series of related miniature explosions as doomed moths are noisily incinerated in the flame of a lethal porch lantern suspended above Quilty's head at the Enchanted Hunters. If the symbolism is heavy-handed, the image that delivers it is really quite elegant. Here at last Adrian Lyne has put his fondness for beautiful imagery and striking set pieces in the service of something of substance. And at the heart of it all is a substantial Lolita too, embodied for the second time in a movie, and this time with great feeling. She is surely realized as well as Humbert's darling is ever likely to be in any visual medium.

If Dominique Swain's performance as Dolores Haze is really a joint venture between her and Adrian Lyne, both parties can be proud of it. Swain looked just right: she was a reddish brunette with mobility between plainness and beauty, the possessor of child-like innocence and a devilish sense of mischief. A natural atten-tion grabber, Swain had an ebullience that had to be harnessed, not suppressed. There is little doubt from Lyne's characteristically diplomatic comments that she could be a handful on set, occasion-ally exasperating both leading man and director, but in general she seems to have been a remarkably mature fourteen-year-old who knew that her love of being the center of the action came with a price tag, and in this case it involved toeing the line.

From her first scene, lying prone reading a movie book on a summer lawn, her dress rendered translucent by a grass sprinkler, Swain inhabits Lolita with extraordinary confidence. Whether teasing Humbert, fighting with Charlotte, or insouciantly using the Ramsdale home lavatory with the door open, she looks absolutely right in those early scenes. Later, when Lolita is promoted from stepdaughter to lover, Swain's ability to switch emotional gear is remarkable, as is her projection of Lolita's strategic deployment of her newfound power. To watch her extracting favors from Humbert with calculated entreaties that segue from the playful to the whor-ish is both disturbing and hypnotic to watch. It is also diverting to contrast her physical movement on the tennis court (by accident or design, this is a good approximation of Lolita's blend of natural grace and clumsy technique from the athletic Swain) with her real-life lack of coordination when it comes to dancing along to music.

For readers of the novel, Lolita was of course always alive, even if sometimes the only evidence might be the cloud of her warm breath on the cold glass of Humbert's prose. On the screen she has to live independently as well, and in a project dogged by bad luck and extraordinary bad timing, Dominique Swain proved to be the movie's major stroke of good fortune.

What would Vladimir Nabokov have thought of her and this film? We cannot know, but the best clue comes from the one person who might plausibly stand in for him—his son Dmitri. As noted earlier, Dmitri Nabokov has enjoyed a prodigiously talented and cultured life, in addition to which, by general assent, he has triumphantly fulfilled the role of being his father's ideal translator. In his addtional function as the executor of his father's estate he has always been a fiercely protective upholder of standards, both literary and moral. Although the unending stream of literary and copyright assaults may have occasionally found him wanting in streetwise instincts, Dmitri Nabokov has never been short of custodial vigor. He elected to assist on Lyne's film and was by all accounts a supportive consultant, apart from the odd complaint that had more to do with literalism than literary license. He protested, for example, that Humbert's car was the "wrong" make, and Lyne thought he was simply comparing it with the car in which the young Dmitri and his parents had crisscrossed the States on his father's summer butterfly hunts. Yet Dmitri Nabokov was quite right: according to the novel the car should have been some make of sedan, not a 1940s Ford DeLuxe with timber-side frames and doors. Even so, the model of car used was an inspired choice for the film; with its wood trim and its waffle array of ceiling pigeonholes for stashing maps and papers, it has an organic look that corresponds well to its role as a (quite literal) mobile home for Humbert and Lolita.

In 1997, Lyne rather nervously screened the finished film for Dmitri Nabokov, who pronounced it "stunning" and subsequently wrote a fulsome endorsement.

"The new *Lolita* is a sensitively conceived, beautifully produced film," he wrote. "Far from being the explicit shocker some feared and others craved, it achieves a cinematic dimension of poetry far closer to the novel than Stanley Kubrick's distant approximation. Lyne's *Lolita* . . . tend(s) to let the viewer's fancy fend for itself, as Nabokov's prose did for the reader. . . . The latest *Lolita* is splendid."

Left: a very wholesome Lolita (Sue Lyon) says good-bye to Humbert (James Mason) before setting off for summer camp in Stanley Kubrick's bid to cinematize Nabokov's novel. (*Lolita*, 1962, MGM). Right: Dominique Swain as Lolita regards the dark presence of Humbert (Jeremy Irons) with a suitable expression of mistrust. (*Lolita*, 1997, Showtime/Pathé)

[12]

BLOOD SISTERS:

Some Responses to *Lolita*

VLADIMIR NABOKOV FINISHED WRITING *LOLITA* ON DECEMBER 6, 1953. In France earlier that same year, Françoise Quoirez, the eighteen-year-old daughter of a wealthy Parisian industrialist, had just failed her examinations at the Sorbonne and subsequently spent the summer writing a novella. She decided to call it *Bonjour Tristesse* and herself Sagan after Princesse de Sagan in Proust's *À la recherche du temps perdu*. Her book was published in 1954. Its success was considerable and international, and by 1959 it had sold 850,000 copies in France alone.

Françoise Sagan had cast herself as Cécile, a spoiled seventeen-year-old whose intimate relationship with her forty-year-old Don Juan of a father seemed to have all but one of the characteristics of an incestuous affair. On an extended summer vacation with him at a villa in the Riviera, she amuses herself by playing malicious cupid as Daddy juggles two women: an empty-headed young mistress whom he believes helps him cling to his vanishing youth and a more mature woman who perhaps ought to suit him better. As her father prepares to announce that he is at last taking the sensible course, Cécile, with a recently acquired summer boyfriend of her own, petulantly manipulates everyone like chess pieces, conspiring to make the woman her father now intends to marry believe that he is deceiving her. This causes the distraught woman to drive blindly from the villa to die in the kind of portentous road accident often featured in books like this. Cécile's harsh discovery that her game has resulted in irreversible tragedy is presented as a moral awakening and a rite of passage rolled into one. She starts out sounding like an old child, winds up sounding like a young woman; the collateral damage is one dead body. The book's title, taken from a poem by Paul Éluard, means "hello, sadness."

Sagan's book scandalized family-loving France because of the iconoclastic attitudes behind this story of a daddy's girl for whom sex was a game and traditional notions of love and marriage represented nothing more than routine and boredom. Tame as it may seem now, *Bonjour Tristesse* also rang alarm bells because it was a precocious broadside from a member of a young generation whose growing cultural clout threatened to spread far beyond the realm of pop music and fashion. The intimate father-daughter relationship added an extra sense of illicit danger, but perhaps most shockingly of all, the book was written by an obviously experienced young girl who seemed to know a great deal about sex and power.

When *Lolita* was published in the United States four years later, the initial outcry, of course, centered on the scandalous sexual relationship between a middle-aged man and a little girl. Then gradually a subsidiary source of outrage emerged. Harder to caricature— or perhaps even to recognize at first—it was to add a new subtext to the Lolita effect. "It was not so much the idea of an adult having sexual designs on a child that was appalling," wrote media critic Marie Winn. "It was Lolita herself, unvirginal long before Humbert came upon the scene, so knowing, so jaded, so unchildlike, who seemed to violate something America held sacred."

Bonjour Tristesse and *Lolita* have almost nothing in common apart from having both made their debuts in the midfifties and sharing any sociological similarities we may choose to infer from each. Their telling difference, though, is that Sagan's narrator relates everything from a very young woman's point of view, while Nabokov's Humbert is a middle-aged male who allows his leading lady no real voice of her own. The controlling effect of Humbert's oppressive viewpoint was to feature in forty years of feminist discussion about *Lolita*, in which the most commonly recurring complaint was that we simply never get to hear the girl's point of view—she is effectively gagged by the man in charge. The wider implications of this in a male-dominated society, for those who wanted to point them out, were resonant with accusation.

In any case, from time to time, Dolores Haze would, so to speak, try to find her voice and get her version of things published, even though Dmitri Nabokov staunchly resisted most authors' eager efforts to infringe his father's copyright by reanimating Lo in order to hear what she might have to say. Postmodernism, however, had changed the cultural landscape and had thrown up in its wake a succession of parodies, commentaries, and borrowings right across the media spectrum. From the playfully nostalgic architectural quotations of Philip Johnson, through populist TV faux-nostalgia like *Happy Days*, to the retro-allusive movies of the Coen Brothers, the past (or at least the reimagined past) was often where the future seemed to lie. It was therefore a short step from plays like Tom Stoppard's refocused exploration of the court of the prince of Denmark, *Rosencrantz & Guildenstern Are Dead* (1966) to Alice Randall's *The Wind Done Gone* (2001)—*Gone with the Wind* retold by Scarlett O'Hara's black half sister. It was further inevitable, copyright restrictions notwithstanding, that some reborn literary

Lolitas might eventually make it through the courts—or at least sidestep them—and get into print.

The most infamous bid came in 1995 in the form of a first novel from Italian journalist and translator Pia Pera. Titled *Lo's Diary*, it is a distinctly curious novel. Setting out to retell the familiar plot of *Lolita* from its title character's point of view, in doing so it expands and embellishes her story by means of strangely unsympathetic insights into her character. In Pera's book, Dolores Schlegel, née Maze, does not perish in a remote Northwest territory but lives on into adulthood and actually turns up in person at a fictionalized Olympia Press in Paris, accompanied by deaf husband Dick, during a visit to the French capital. Working at this reconstituted Olympia is John Ray Jr., the original novel's foreword writer to whom Dolores gives her own "childish" diary as a corrective to Humbert's version of things. Humbert's "real" name is now revealed as Humbert Guibert. "Maybe you'd take a look at my own impressions of that time," she says, handing over the diary to the bemused Ray. "They're definitely less literary."

They definitely are. Her diary is not taken up by Olympia, and the Schlegels depart Paris before John Ray can return the diary to her. He eventually leaves his job at the publishing house, and when he goes he takes the scrappy memoir with him. Only in 1995 does he finally edit and publish it, whereupon we learn that Lolita, in Pera's hands, certainly does have a voice, even if it sounds suspiciously like the voice of a forty-two-year-old Italian woman working in the same medium—but hardly at the same level—as Vladimir Nabokov.

Pera's Lolita is a child assembled to realize unclear literary ambitions, a twelve- or thirteen-year-old girl of the late 1940s with an impossibly sophisticated writing style and a tendency to incorporate into her diary musings that clearly derive from an adult sensibility acquired during a later period of twentieth-century history.

Any expectation that there might emerge a Lolita sympathetically informed by a perceptive feminist awareness seems doomed to disappointment. In short, Dolores Maze comes across as being gratuitously unpleasant even before Humbert gets his hooks into her.

The book was written in Italian and translated into English by Anna Goldstein, but even making allowances for the inherent problems of translation, this Lolita's thoughts are rendered in a vernacular considerably less authentic-sounding than Nabokov's laboriously researched attempts to reproduce the speech patterns of American kids of the 1940s. If he only occasionally sounded a false note, Pera hardly ever hits a true one. The following scarcely believable exchange between Lolita and her mother (and presumably dutifully reproduced by the twelve-year-old in her diary) gives some idea.

Wanting to dissuade Lolita from becoming an actress so that she can train as a nuclear physicist (!), Mom says:

"I don't like to think of you as an actress—the most that can happen is you end up on the poster of the atomic mushroom like that Spanish illiterate Hayworth."

"And nuclear physics?"

"You might still become the first woman to make a bomb so perfect that it would kill the enemy without destroying a single city. Wouldn't you like that?"

No doubt a suitably diligent professor of semiotics somewhere might try to interpret that absurd exchange with the nuggets that Rita Hayworth (born Margarita Cansino) was given the middle name of Carmen, that she was sexually abused by her father, and that her image was affixed to the first atomic bomb (all true facts), but nothing can breathe life into such a contrived exchange.

Of the plot it can be said that *Lo's Diary* spans the pre-Humbertian days in Ramsdale (now rechristened Goatscreek), to the point when Lolita finally leaves Humbert to start a life of her own.

This Lolita's wit is spiteful, her sexual knowledge improbably comprehensive, and her viewpoint very unchildlike. Despite repeated reference to the novelty of atomic power, there is little or no textural period detail to set the scene. Pera's treatment of a single famous episode typifies her book's strangely gratuitous tendency to demonize Lolita and conjure highly doubtful scenarios. The incident that Humbert presents as his desperately skillful attempt to achieve sexual gratification by bouncing Lolita up and down on his lap to music without her having any idea of what he is doing comes over rather differently here. Nabokov had Lolita clutching "a banal, Eden-red apple" at the start of the scene—the apple's accidental and heavy-handed symbolism being parodied as part and parcel of its description. Pera has the twelve-year-old girl—not Humbert—initiate what we might call (with an infelicity to match Pera's own sometimes anachronistic language) "the lap-dancing scene." Yes, twelve-year-old Lolita Maze intentionally equips herself with a red apple to match her lipstick because "lipstick by itself isn't enough: the attack has to come from multiple directions" and concludes "no man can resist a woman who has an apple in her hand. It's theological."

Prior to *Lo's Diary* the open-minded may have allowed that Lolita was an unusually bold flirt or even a coconspirator in the above scene, but to cast her as its Machiavellian creator seems absurd. Throughout, *Lo's Diary* runs similarly dreary attempts to depict Lolita as a sexual punk for the postwar years, a crude protofeminist given to expressing opinions like "You have to keep a firm hand on a man, just like a horse," and a budding sadist who tortures her pet hamster to death, heaps unremitting abuse and hatred on her "Shitmom" Isabel (as Charlotte is redubbed), and decides to ensnare Humbert Guibert as "Daddy 2" from the moment they first meet in the garden of 341 Grassy Street.

To readers very familiar with *Lolita* there is perhaps a certain morbid fun to be had in seeing which of the book's scenes are revisited from the viewpoint of this newly vicious and venomous Lolita, but in the end *Lo's Diary* comes over as a rather sterile conceit with a lifeless narrator working to an obscure purpose. It is a shame, because all those voices calling out for Lolita's point of view might reasonably have expected something better, or at least something more interesting. The final irony is of course that we learned far more about Lolita from Humbert the Unreliable than we ever do from Pera's ventriloquist's dummy. Even so, there is some small redeeming merit in the book's final stages that, while lacking the Dickensian drama of a murder, a death in captivity, and a death in childbirth, do convey Lolita's awful sense of emptiness before she slips away with Clare Quilty (here renamed Gerry Sue Filthy) to start living a life of her own. The lack of dramatic resolution may be anticlimactic, but it does, in an odd way, chime with the real-life experiences of both Sally Horner and Natascha Kampusch. Like Horner, this Lolita has been in occasional telephone contact with a friend on the other side of the country but has somehow never got around to telling her the full story until now. As in Kampusch's case, when escape comes in *Lo's Diary*, there seems to be no particular reason why it should not have come earlier or, for that matter, later. It must simply have been that the time was right, not merely the opportunity available. This hint of plausibility is hardly enough to redeem what has gone before, either in terms of literature or presenting a believable, articulate Lolita to the world, but it would be churlish to deny that it is compensation of sorts.

As long as *Lo's Diary* remained an Italian-language book the Nabokov estate did not take legal action, but when it ventured into English translation Dmitri Nabokov became more militant. Eventually a compromise was reached; it was agreed that a portion of the English book's proceeds should go to the International PEN Club for literary philanthropic use, while Dmitri Nabokov would get to insert a brief preemptive preface into the English edition of *Lo's*

Diary. That preface ventures as close as it can to being a scathing review while ostensibly seeking to set out the sanctity of copyright in general and the legal history of this borrowing in particular.

In 1999 came another borrowed fiction, its aim quite openly set out by its author: "This novel is in part a literary parody of that great work by Vladimir Nabokov, *Lolita*," wrote Emily Prager. "This is my reply to both the book and to the icon that the character Lolita has become."

Prager's *Roger Fishbite* comes as a great relief after *Lo's Diary.* Very funny (there were no intentional laughs in Pera's book), effortlessly well written, and a tacitly admitted diversion rather than a Novel with a Serious Purpose, it also illustrates just how different a contemporary Lolita needs to be to make any sense at all. As Stephen Schiff noted, what Kubrick actually created and Adrian Lyne seemed seriously to have contemplated—an updated Lolita—automatically compromises Nabokov's little girl because she was inseparably a child of her time. Transplanted to the late 1950s by Kubrick, she was merely culturally marooned, but teleported to the end of the twentieth century or the start of the twenty-first, she would have to become something else entirely—a Hayley Stark from *Hard Candy* or, in this case, a Lucky Lady Linderhof from Manhattan.

Roger Fishbite is set in the 1990s, Lucky Lady Linderhof is Prager's triple-palate-tripping Dolores Haze, and this memoir is driven by a plot that places a witty distorting mirror in front of *Lolita.* The Lolita and Humbert roles are partially reversed, and this child-heroine lives a perfectly believable life in the knowing modern world of Oprah Winfrey, dysfunctional families, ubiquitous computers, the *National Enquirer,* Disney, and MTV. Humbert's ladies and gentlemen of the jury becomes Lucky's "Dear readers and Watchers of tabloid TV and press." By the time she is fourteen, Lucky does not aspire to be an actress, as her original did, but instead yearns one day to have her own confessional TV show ("*Babytalk*

starring Lucky Lady Linderhof. And now your hostess, Lucky Lady!
... Thank you. Thank you very much and welcome to today's show:
Controllable Molesters").

Lucky does try to imitate the mannerisms of a certain film
actress, although her model is Veronica Lake ("careful and precise
and slow like honey") who died in 1973 and whom she can therefore only know through old movies on TV. What is more, privately
educated Lucky knows all about Lewis Carroll and Alice Liddell
and concludes that the author probably did molest the muse of his
great children's book ("I'd say yes from the sad look on her face in
the photogravures"), yet philosophically young Lucky weighs the
moral balance: "But he wrote her such a great story. . . . Is the innocence of one girl so important next to *Alice in Wonderland*? Does it
matter if it wasn't quote soooo wonderful for her? A hundred years
of beautifully bound editions? Can anyone honestly say they would
save the child and lose the book?" This thought, intentionally or
otherwise, reverses the sentiment of a 1925 Russian poem by Vladimir Nabokov, "The Mother," that explored weeping Mary's grief
after the execution of Jesus.

> What if her son had stayed home with her,
> And carpentered and sung? What if those tears
> Cost more than redemption?

While still a preteen, living in Manhattan with a dipsomaniac
mother who currently has a new man in her life—Roger Fishbite—
Lucky Linderhof is precociously intelligent, attends a very classy
school, and is quite prepared to help out any less educated readers by
translating the French phrases she studiously drops into her memoir
as she goes along. Lucky is of course showing off but slips up only
once, gilding the lily to unintentional comic effect: "He leaped back
in mock fright [mock—that means faux, which is French for fake]."

Lucky's takes on some of Humbert's bits of woolgathering are often very good. To his speculation, "Are all girl children nymphets?" she offers, "Is every man a dirty old man? Oh no! Were that true then little girls would have no rest and certainly go mad."

Prager's version of the famous Humbert lap scene is bracingly casual and brief. Hunky Texan daddy-to-be Roger Fishbite sits Lucky on his lap ("Which was not all that comfortable for some reason," her memoir reports insouciantly), but Mom immediately interrupts them and starts bossing her new beau about, prompting the following thought from her daytime TV aficionado daughter: "'Spineless Men—Can You Change Them?'—the answer was no. Montel Williams Show #50, September of last year."

As the plot develops the role reversal is very artfully managed, and the modern setting allows Lucky to manipulate Fishbite in quite believable ways. He is still the oppressor, but this is a more equal contest and one that could never have been played out in those dingy motels strung out from New England to New Mexico (in a nice revision, Fishbite takes Lucky on a brisk tour of airport hotels, surely today's most characterless hostelries). Suddenly motherless, Lucky succumbs to sex but keeps the precocious upper hand for a while: "It was still oral sex, which the ancients called cunnilingus or rabbit's tongue if you are good at languages as I am." Smarter than her oppressor, she can push all the right buttons to taunt him, but she still cannot change the balance of power. Dramatizing the exploitation of child workers in Third World countries by famous-label companies gives Lucky and her school friends a related child-enslavement cause to pursue. A chance encounter with some dolled-up young girls at a beauty pageant being held at a hotel gives Fishbite his Camp Kewattommie moment and lets Lucky chat to some of her less privileged contemporaries. It seems they know all about JonBenet Ramsey and are generally philosophical about the tiresome attentions of men: "They can't help it," said Mary Jane. "We look so beautiful, like little candy women or something."

Prager's opening dedication, celebrating the "boundless determination and unstoppable joy" of "all the little girls I've met who started out in desperate circumstances" sets the tone for a very satisfying neo-Lolita, full of sparkiness and bright wit, who reveals some touching gaps in her otherwise precociously sophisticated appreciation of the world. Lucky suffers the same sexual abuse that Lolita did but eventually takes justice into her own hands and, for her crime, is awarded her own afternoon TV show, weekdays at four, even before she is released from the New York Department of Correction, Juvenile Division. It all sounds horribly plausible, and through it all Lucky Linderhof shines, making a welcome late entry to the line of Lolitas that by now stretches right down the hall leading back to Ithaca, New York, where the first production model was so exquisitely assembled.

If Lolita represented, as Nabokov once wrote, a "warm glow," an enduring, comforting presence in his oeuvre, *Roger Fishbite* is perhaps best described a splendid firework, fizzing and dazzling and then gone. But feisty Lucky Linderhof still seems a genuine if distant blood relation of Lolita Haze. Her fate is different only because the times are different, and because the times are different, Lucky Lady is well named. No Gray Star postnatal complications for her.

– – –

Less lucky and even more distant relations of Lolita have always been a staple of literature. In recent years some women authors have brought particularly chilling insights and perspectives to sadly familiar scenarios featuring girl-child victims. A. M. Homes's *The End of Alice* seems at its start to be promising some sort of evenhanded correspondence or dialog between a nineteen-year-old woman and an imprisoned male pedophile, but things soon turn out to be disturbingly otherwise. Alice Sebold's *The Lovely Bones* gives an exclusive authorial voice to a raped and murdered fourteen-year-old girl who views the earthly aftershocks of her life and death from a personal heaven. One of the most unexpected Lolita spin-offs, however, was neither a borrowing nor a variant; it was not even, strictly speaking, a fiction. It was a celebration in the form of a memoir in which fictional Western women—among them Elizabeth Bennet, Catherine Sloper, Daisy Buchanan, Emma Bovary, Daisy Miller, and Dolores Haze—were introduced to real Eastern women in a weekly discussion group surreptitiously held in the capital city of the Islamic Republic of Iran, right at the end of the twentieth century.

Reading Lolita in Tehran: A Memoir in Books is Azar Nafisi's account of an undercover book discussion group she organized for a handful of female students after resigning her teaching post at Iran's University of Allameh Tabtabai. Born in the old Iran in the days of the shah but educated in England and the United States, Nafisi had returned to teach in her native country in the late 1970s, just in time for the Iranian Revolution, the rise of Ayatollah Khomeini, and, among other things most unwelcome from her point of view, a sustained erosion of personal liberties that proved especially harsh for women. Nafisi was first fired from the University of Tehran in 1981 for refusing to wear the veil and ultimately given no option but to resign from Allameh Tabtabai by the ever more rigorous restrictions placed upon what she could teach there. Allameh Tabtabai still had a reputation as the country's most liberal university at the time, but all things are comparative and she found the university regime intolerable. So the secretive book group was in effect a gift from an international academic to seven of her brightest female students. It took place covertly on Thursday mornings at Nafisi's home, a sanctuary where those young women could shed not only their outdoor robes and scarves to reveal a lively selection of jeans, T-shirts, and other informal items worn beneath but also divest themselves of any restrictions forbidding what they might discuss. They used the sessions, guided by Nafisi, to discuss the unique potency of literature, as well as comparing and contrasting the travails of some of fiction's most memorable heroines with their own lives and straitened circumstances.

Of all the books discussed—and these included those by Henry James, F. Scott Fitzgerald, Jane Austen, and Gustave Flaubert—the signature work for the whole enterprise was Nabokov's *Lolita*. If it seems strange for such an embattled group of women to have embraced a hard-to-get book that had inflamed public opinion even in comparatively liberal America, it was not quite as it seemed. Looked at another way, *Lolita* was the natural defining novel for the book-reading exercise. In the Islamic Republic of Iran, where the age of consent had been summarily lowered from eighteen to nine, the sense of shock about a middle-aged man having sex with a twelve-year-old girl was, shall we say, considerably less potent than in most Western countries. The *Lolita* that Nafisi introduced to her students was for them in essence a story about tyranny and disenfranchisement. That the book was also the epitome of Nabokov's own definition of art—"beauty plus pity"—only added humanity and pleasure to what was for Nafisi's students an all too recognizable plight.

If Nafisi's purplish prose occasionally seems to reflect a little too much preoccupation with her own role—the sweet drama of a liberal academic who chooses to remain in a tyrannical society—she becomes an unimpeachable commentator when addressing Lolita, which she obviously adores, and talking about *Lolita* herself, whose plight she clearly finds heartbreaking.

To the most rebellious of her students, a young woman she calls Yassi, Nafisi explains that "the desperate truth of Lolita's story is *not* the rape of a twelve-year-old by a dirty old man, but the confiscation of one individual's life by another." She goes on to argue that, although we cannot know what Lolita's life might have been like had Humbert not hijacked it, "the novel, the finished work, is hopeful, beautiful even, a defense not just of beauty but of life, ordinary everyday life, all the normal pleasures that Lolita, like Yassi, was deprived of."

Nafisi consistently refuses to force *Lolita* into the role of crude political parable about regimes like that of the Islamic Republic but still insists the book goes "against the grain" of all totalitarian beliefs. She sees surprising parallels too. Lolita's pre-Humbertian past is shown to us in the novel only in glimmers, pinholes of light penetrating the fabric of Humbert's narrative. Much of that past has to do with loss—the loss of a father and baby brother—but a loss sustained early in life can sometimes seem like nothing more than a neutral absence, and Nafisi argues in parallel that her students, having never lived in a more liberal prerevolutionary Iran, do not so much miss what they never had as labor valiantly under its nonexistence. What is more, like Lolita, who was reinvented by Humbert to replace long-lost Annabel and fulfill a very specific role in his own life, Nafisi's students also suffer the fate of playing out roles in someone else's fantasy rather than determining their own lives. They too have been blamed and punished when failing to conform to the self-serving roles imposed upon them by fixated men. ("Philistines," Vladimir Nabokov once declared during a rare filmed interview, "are ready-made souls in plastic bags." He was a lifelong enemy of "poshlust," a Russian word connoting the pretentiously vulgar, sentimental, banal, or sham.)

"Like the best defense attorneys . . . Humbert exonerates himself by implicating his victim—a method we are quite familiar with in the Islamic Republic of Iran," writes Nafisi. "Of course, all murderers and oppressors have a long list of grievances about their victims, only most are not as eloquent as Humbert Humbert."

In truth, Nafisi dominates the book discussions, offering her interpretations to her students and imposing shape on the activities. Her flock, meanwhile, is limited to coming up with interesting but dislocated opinions about the various aspects of Lolita that resonate with them. One points out that some critics seem to treat the book the same way Humbert treated Lolita: "They only see themselves and what they want to see." Responding to the scene where Lolita suddenly weeps to see fat little Avis hug her dad, the student called Nassrin says, "It is interesting that Nabokov, who is so hard on poshlust, would make us pity the loss of the most conventional forms of life."

Another student is genuinely puzzled by what she sees as a paradox: why does reading a tragic story like *Lolita* (or *Madame Bovary*, for that matter) make us happy? Nafisi replies, after due professorial thought, that the paradox is only an illusion: if every great work of art is "an act of insubordination against the betrayals, horrors, and infidelities of life," then that is what makes us happy and that is why "we greedily read *Lolita* as our heart breaks for its small, vulgar, poetic, and defiant orphaned heroine."

Reading Lolita in Tehran goes on to intertwine the group's own lives with those of some other fictional characters dreamed up by the literary world's inspired insubordinates. Like the cabins at Camp Q (each named after a Disney creature, diligent readers of the novel will recall), this book's subsequent sections are named for Jay Gatsby, F. Scott Fitzgerald, Henry James, and Jane Austen, itself a sequence that nicely blurs the boundaries between invented people and real ones. The triumph of Azar Nafisi's book, however, lies not in its art but in its heart. Margaret Atwood called it "a literary life raft on Iran's fundamentalist sea," and Nafisi herself saw the covert book meetings that inspired it as part of the many pleasures of life to be savored all the more for being forbidden. The mainspring of the exercise, however, was its author's precise understanding and passionate appreciation of *Lolita* as a living thing, an organism within which exists another living thing, a little girl who can surely touch any good reader in any society.

"'It is hard for me,' Mahshid said . . . , 'to read the parts about Lolita's feelings. All she wants is to be a normal girl.'"

A more astringent response to *Lolita* came from the Canadian writer Justine Brown. Her winning recollection of being introduced to the book in the hope that it would be a subtle monitory experience only goes to demonstrate the dangers of trying to use art as a moral compass.

"I wept bitterly when I first read Vladimir Nabokov's *Lolita*," Brown recalled.

A lady named Carol, who parachuted into my life like a '70s Mary Poppins and quickly became a friend, slipped me the book. In retrospect, I see a warning featured prominently: be aware. She presented the book by way of proscription—to alert me to the erotic power of nubiles and the pitfalls of that power, to the magnetism of 12-year-old girls, for some men. It was 1977, I was 12 and so was Brooke Shields. *Pretty Baby* was shedding its soft *Penthouse* glow in movie houses around the world, and Roman Polanski would soon be on the run, leaving his adolescent lover in disarray. We had our brown limbs, our cut-offs and halter tops; we had our ice cream and lip gloss. Advice was in order, but Carol was too subtle for that. (Others were more direct: "Now everyone will want to screw you," remarked one of the grown-ups bracingly.)

Carol gave me a copy of *Lolita* instead of a sermon. And that is how I came to read it, in two rainy summer afternoons, when I was 12. And when I emerged tearfully from the bedroom, she just nodded and opened her arms, for I was a sensitive kid. "Poor, poor Humbert!" I cried. "Lolita was so mean!"

- - -

Despite the young Justine Brown's unexpected loyalties and Pia Pera's dubious advocacy, Lolita Haze has usually found her most sympathetic champions in women. None of them has been more quietly persuasive than Vladimir Nabokov's extraordinary wife and collaborator Véra. The acute accent on the e, by the way, was a rare instance of her own literary invention. She added it to help with the correct pronunciation of her name when the Nabokovs first moved to America—it is Vay-rah, not Veer-a. Otherwise, Véra Nabokov, née Slonim, a highly cultured Russian Jew, a great beauty with a sophisticated taste in literature and a talent for languages, wrote hardly anything but diaries and letters, dedicating her life to the role of uber-assistant to a husband whose legendary absent-mindedness and impracticality in the real world contrasted comically with his genius at creating and organizing exquisitely detailed fantasy worlds.

Véra was an aristocratic woman who made a dramatic escape from Bolshevik Russia in 1920, eventually arriving in that émigrés' favorite city, Berlin, where she was still to be found supporting husband Vladimir and young son Dmitri as late as 1938, a date whose resonance now makes this sound like an insanely risky dalliance for a Jewish woman. She was the life partner who battled with publishers when the Nabokovs lived in poverty and the one who beat off the unwanted fans when *Lolita* made her husband notorious. She was the steel-willed woman who carried the licensed handgun when they toured remote territories on entomological excursions. She was the practical one who drove their Oldsmobile in a mixed spirit of exhilaration and heroic martyrdom because Vladimir could not drive at all. ("I have upwards of 200,000 miles under my belt," she wrote in a letter to a friend in the early 1960s, "but each time I get behind the wheel I hand my soul over to God.") She typed everything Vladimir wrote. She delivered his lectures at Cornell when he was too ill to do it himself. Without her, there would have been no *Lolita*; many who knew the couple went so far as to say that without her, there would have been no Vladimir Nabokov. Asked once in an interview if he could say how important his wife had been to him, Nabokov, a man who calculated the precise meaning of every word he used, answered simply, "No, I could not."

Véra not only enabled a great literary career, she literally saved *Lolita*'s life when she snatched the novel's pages from a sacrificial bonfire started by her husband in the yard of a rented house in East Seneca Street in Ithaca. There were to be several subsequent bids at immolation by an author beset with what he saw as insurmountable doubts about his masterwork, but the first and most famous attempt had a witness, one of Nabokov's own students, a senior named Dick Keegan who had surely been handed a poisoned chalice when he was recruited as his professor's personal driving instructor. (This exercise was an unqualified disaster; it remains one of American literature's great ironies that the man who created that magnificent road trip right in the center of that magnificent novel was always utterly unable to master the controls of an automobile.) So it was Keegan who happened to see Nabokov start to feed pages of *Lolita* into a galvanized incinerator in the yard one morning. Véra suddenly appeared from the house and commanded "Get away from there!" and started stamping out some smoldering pages. "We are keeping this."

She was also the woman who, on May 20, 1958, started to maintain a diary in which, to begin with, her own entries and those of her husband were closely intertwined, a calligraphic synthesis of their inseparable lives together. Gradually though, Véra became the sole diarist at a time when *Lolita* was all the rage. It was as though she sensed that this would be a pivotal time in their lives, the breakthrough, the start of financial independence for them, and a benign bouleversement well worth recording at the time that it was actually happening. Also, Vladimir had entertained vague ambitions to write a comic article for *The New Yorker* about the trials and tribulations of *Lolita*'s publication, so it is possible that Véra's notes might have been designed to help inform that. Yet a more personal tone emerges in this rare instance of Véra seemingly writing as herself rather than as her husband's coconspirator and administrative alter ego.

All of which is by way of setting the scene for Véra's resonant thoughts on Lolita—not the book, but the little girl. The following passage comes from that diary (it was therefore a private opinion and not intended as some public broadside at the critics) and represents her response to what she felt had been an unfair assessment of the book's heroine. Critics, Véra felt, were too ready to discuss the book in terms of signs, symbols, and moral stances, too willing also to recognize the pathos in Humbert while dismissing Lolita as little more than a libidinous brat.

"I wish," wrote Véra, "someone would notice the tender description of the child's helplessness, her pathetic dependence upon the monstrous HH, and her heartrending courage all along, culminating in that squalid but essentially pure and healthy marriage, and her letter, and her dog. And that terrible expression on her face when she had been cheated by HH out of some little pleasure that had been promised. They all miss the fact that 'the horrid little brat' Lolita is essentially very good indeed—or she would not have straightened out after being crushed so terribly, and found a decent life with poor Dick more to her liking than the other kind."

Véra's humane and touching observation elegantly returns us to our starting point: that all too often Lolita got bad press even before her name became every third-rate tabloid editor's sluttish embodiment of female teenage libido and every huckster's instant insurance for sexing up the shabbiest trinket.

CONCLUSION

FOR THOSE OF US WHO HAVE SPENT ALL OF OUR ADULT LIVES PLEA-surably haunted by the literary presence that is *Lolita*, it is impossible to encounter anything from the slightest echo of her name to the most direct reference without giving an involuntary smile of recognition. Whenever the credits roll on a movie featuring Canadian actress Lolita Davidovich, there is Lo suddenly supplied with a somehow felicitous Russian-sounding patronym.

In Jim Jarmusch's movie *Broken Flowers* (2005), a raunchy young girl parades herself naked in front of a stranger (Bill Murray) who has called at the house to see her mother, who is out. He asks her name. "Lolita," she replies insouciantly, and the middle-aged caller can only repeat the name in dry disbelief. The association is lost on her. She is too young. He smiles.

A flickering half-century-old episode of a once-famous British comedy show, *Hancock's Half Hour*, is reshown on TV. As its lugubrious hero leaves his local public library—the setting for the episode—he asks, with little hope, "No sign of *Lolita* yet?" "No," comes the usual answer. The moment, preserved on a kinescope, simultaneously reflects the book's mainstream fame, the long waiting lists of people who wanted to borrow it from their local library, and the fact that, after all the fuss, *Lolita* was never prosecuted or banned in Britain at all.

At the time of this writing a Bollywood movie, *Nishabd* (2007), has just been released. It is advertised as a remake of the 1962 *Lolita*, and rumor has it that Indian audiences have not warmed to the film. Another smile.

There are musical triggers too. Judy Holliday's voice and ukulele rendition of "Dolores" in *The Marrying Kind* (1952) reprises a Frank Sinatra novelty hit from the 1940s. Lolita's given name, and the roses, and the comically contrived rhymes might have amused Humbert, the impromptu lyricist of "Little Carmen," if only he had paid as much attention to what came out of those gorgeous, nickel-eating Wurlitzers as he did to what went into them.

> From a balcony above me, she whispers "Love me,"
>   and throws a rose.
> Ah, but she is twice as lovely as the rose she throws.
>
> I would die to be with my Dolores, aye-aye-aye Dolores,
> I was made to serenade Dolores, chorus after chorus.

And so on.

Martha Wainwright has a song called "Lolita" containing the lines "'Cause me and Hummy / we understand each other we got the same problem / you and Lolita." Meanwhile, Lolita prototype Annabel Lee actually made it into a number of popular songs. I remember once doing a kind of aural double take when hearing, on a Nashville radio station, Waylon Jennings singing the words, "I was a child / And she was a child." This turned out to be "Beautiful Annabel Lee," Harlan Howard's country reworking of the famous poem. Poe's original verse has also been featured, either as a song or a narration, on albums by everyone from Jim Reeves to Lou Reed.

Histoire de Melody Nelson was a themed album from French singer-songwriter Serge Gainsbourg in 1971 and is generally accepted to have been inspired by *Lolita*. Melody is an androgynous fifteen-year-old red-haired girl whom Gainsbourg's alter ego accidentally knocks off her bicycle with his Rolls-Royce. He takes her to a hotel to recover and promptly seduces her in one of its rococo bedrooms. Soon accident-prone Melody will die in a mystical plane crash over New Guinea, and, as Jean-François Brieu's album liner notes rather colorfully put it, "Between these two blood lettings, she will be deflowered by the hero: a little trickle of hemoglobin, tribute paid to an initiation into pleasure" (the translation from French is mine but the sanguinary imagery is Brieu's). The sumptuous key track of the album, "Ballade de Melody Nelson," was actually recorded before the other songs. It featured vocal interjections from Gainsbourg's English girlfriend, Jane Birkin, who also impersonates Melody on the album sleeve—red wig, rouged cheeks, toy monkey clutched to her bare bosom, and crotch-hugging jeans. She also appeared with Gainsbourg in a twenty-eight-minute 1971 French TV special, *Melody*, directed by Jean-Christophe Averty. It promoted the album in what now looks like a narrative sequence of primitive music videos. Both performers mime, Birkin sports a variety of provocative outfits, and Gainsbourg looks very serious while demonstrating how many different ways it is possible to hold and smoke a cigarette. Kitsch of the highest order, *Melody* the TV special manages to detract from, rather than add to, the drama of the songs. In a pleasing historical coincidence, just as John Barry was finalizing his score for the ill-starred musical *Lolita, My Love*, Vic Flick, erstwhile electric guitarist with the John Barry 7, was one of the British session musicians playing on that 1971 *Melody Nelson* album recorded in post-swinging London. To add a further Nabokovian twist of fate, Jane Birkin had briefly been married to John Barry a few years earlier. In 1975,

Birkin would make her own cult album, *Lolita Go Home*, the title song being a cri de coeur from a nubile schoolgirl badmouthed by women and drooled over by men; it was cowritten by Serge Gainsbourg and Philippe Labro. A year later Birkin would reincarnate a variant of Melody Nelson in Gainsbourg's movie *Je t'aime, moi n'en plus* alongside Joe Dallesandro.

Véra Nabokov, it seems, was once hounded by an unnamed songwriter anxious to secure the rights to Lolita's name for a ballad he had written. His insistence on singing it to her over the phone did not advance his case, which was ultimately refused.

Another smile greeted Martin Amis's 1981 piece for the London *Observer*, "Visiting Mrs Nabokov." The article was remarkable because his account of the encounter at the Montreux Palace Hotel was uncharacteristically deferential. Suddenly unopinionated, the arch prose stylist Amis was for once a starstruck fan, keenly aware of Véra's protectiveness of her late husband's reputation and noting, despite his own careful politeness, that she seemed to always be expecting some appallingly inappropriate interviewer's question. "Mrs. Nabokov, did you ever meet the *real* Lolita?" is his comic example, but he dares voice it only to the reader. The piece was subsequently collected in, and gave its title to, a selection of Amis journalism published in the early 1990s.

Raising a smile too has been the odd encounter of local variants of Bert Stern's Lolita image in poster shops all over the world. The poster is usually displayed in the company of other American classics such as Marilyn Monroe standing over that subway grating, Marlon Brando in his *Wild One* motorcycle leathers, or James Dean from *Giant* standing with a rifle across his shoulders and Elizabeth Taylor at his feet. Sue Lyon too has become a global icon—but of what exactly?

– – –

More familiar but less inclined to raise a smile are two tired old questions that for half a century have tended to come round again and again like visits from an unwelcome friend.

One: was the book a dramatization of Vladimir Nabokov's own sexual proclivities?

Two: doesn't discussing *Lolita*—doesn't the very existence of the book—make pedophilia more socially acceptable?

The second question is so stupid that it does not really deserve an answer, since to confuse discussion with endorsement seems to suggest a complete absence of critical intelligence. It is also perhaps helpful to remember Alfred Hitchcock's response when told that a serial killer had murdered for the third time after seeing *Psycho*: "What movies did he see before the other two?"

The first question is almost as stupid but perhaps deserves two answers, one of them neatly articulated by Azar Nafisi for the benefit of her young Iranian students: "*do not*, under *any* circumstances, belittle a work of fiction by trying to turn it into a carbon copy of real life." The other answer is that while Vladimir Nabokov was undoubtedly flirtatious and had many affairs when young, a 1940s Wellesley junior named Katherine Reese Peebles, under whose spell her Russian professor fell for a while, testified confidently that "he did like young girls. Just not little girls." Peebles and Nabokov had an intimate but short-lived fling, and other than his affair with Irina Yurievna Guadanini in 1930s Paris, this counted as the single biggest threat to the famous Nabokov marriage. Irina was just four years younger than Véra. If Vladimir Nabokov really did like little girls, the best efforts of many diligent biographers have failed to uncover the evidence. In any case, the correct question with regard to any novel is not about personal morality but artistic credibility. Is it possible to depict circumstances and emotions that you have not personally experienced? Well, does anyone ask Hannibal Lecter's creator Thomas Harris how many people he ate by way of injecting credibility into his blockbuster? Was Bret Easton Ellis only able to write *American Psycho* by means of strict empirical research? And what chance would Quentin Tarantino have of remaining at liberty if his films were assumed to be autobiographical? Need we ask? Need we answer?

If you want to tell the truth, write a novel; if you want to tell a lie, write nonfiction. The old adage has much to recommend it. Biography and autobiography have their places, however, perhaps as a branch of fiction that adheres to facts and statistics while animating a lost reality through some sort of art. The present book always seemed to me to want to be a biography of Lolita, in spirit, at least. It could not be one in any literal sense of course, the first and most obvious reason being that Dolores Haze was a fictional character who, to use one of Nabokov's favorite formulations, would not exist at all unless a reader imagined her. On the other hand, many a real-life biographer's subject might argue that the waxwork on the page with whom he or she shares a name is no more "real" than Dolores Haze, Huck Finn, Stanley Kowalski, or Rhett Butler. Writing a biography is a notoriously tricky and subjective business that never fails to offend someone. There can be few more diligently evenhanded biographers than Stacy Schiff, whose book *Véra (Mrs. Vladimir Nabokov)* stands as an elegant example of the genre, yet Ms. Schiff (no relation to Adrian Lyne's scriptwriter, although the name does seem to be a lucky one for Nabokovian projects) has said that "anyone who has ever taken a cat to a vet in a carrying case, and extracted the animal in a blur of claw and hackles and muscle, [knows] what it is to write about Mrs. Nabokov."

The second good reason why Lolita's story cannot really be told as a biography is that we have only one source of information—old unreliable Humbert—and absolutely no corroboration. Yet, perversely, the first prohibition might be considered to negate the second: if Lolita exists only in our imagination (assisted, of course, by a master illusionist with an endless supply of index cards and pencils with erasers), then such a Lolita is surely fair game for all the other fantasies that gradually attach themselves to her name. Admittedly, the artist who created the original might have cause for regret to see his creation embellished by a contingent comprising largely hawkers, impresarios, and assorted opportunists, but the phantom creatures they all conjure are still bona fide inhabitants of the world of human imagination. Every time we choose to believe in one of them instead of the original, it surely tells us something about ourselves and our times. That too I found an interesting aspect of delving into the lives of Lolita: she has been corrupted in a variety of ways, but each corruption tells us something not about her but about us.

Happily, the "real" Lolita can always be perfectly restored for anyone who cares to read or reread Nabokov's novel. That experience is its own high reward as well as the most dependable antidote to the latest brazen, short-skirted, man-eating, teen mutant dreamed up and labeled with the L-word for screen, page, or stage. In this respect I always think about one very haunting scene in the book that acts as a great corrective. (Of course, we all have favorite scenes, sometimes believing that they are somehow ours and that we alone have spotted them; it is an absurd conceit but somehow one that the private deal done between author and reader encourages.) I am thinking of Humbert finding Lolita sitting reading a drama book in an after-hours classroom. The school setting at once sexually arouses him; Lolita sits some way behind the only other person in the room, a little girl the sight of whose white neck and blonde curls further inflames him. Made utterly reckless by this chance opportunity he sits down next to Lolita and purchases, for sixty-five cents and a tawdry promise, the surreptitious grip of her hand on his genitals. Yet almost at once the scene shifts from being provocative to pitiable because of a single brilliant phrase, Nabokov's unmanning description of Lolita's "inky, chalky, red-knuckled hand."

BIBLIOGRAPHY

Albee, Edward. *The Collected Plays of Edward Albee, Vol 3*. Overlook Duckworth, Peter Mayer Publishers, Inc., 2005.

Appel Jr., Alfred. *Nabokov's Dark Cinema*. Oxford University Press, 1974.

Appel Jr., Alfred, and Charles Newman. *Nabokov: Criticism, Reminiscences, Translations and Tributes*. Northwestern University Press, 1970.

Boyd, Brian. *Vladimir Nabokov: The Russian Years*. Princeton University Press, 1990.

Homes, A. M. *The End of Alice*. Transworld Publishers, 1997.

Maar, Michael. *The Two Lolitas*. Verso Books, 2005.

Miller, Henry. *The Air-Conditioned Nightmare*. New Directions, 1981.

Nabokov, Vladimir. *The Enchanter*. Picador, 1987.

Nabokov, Vladimir. *Lolita: A Screenplay*. McGraw-Hill, 1974.

Nabokov, Vladimir. *Poems and Problems*. McGraw-Hill, 1985.

Nabokov, Vladimir. *Speak, Memory*. Penguin, 1951.

Nabokov, Vladimir, and Alfred Appel Jr. *The Annotated Lolita*. Vintage Books, 1991.

Nafisi, Azar. *Reading Lolita in Tehran*. I. B. Tauris, 2003.

Pera, Pia. *Lo's Diary*. Foxrock, Inc., 1999.

Pifer, Ellen, ed. *Vladimir Nabokov's Lolita: A Casebook*. Oxford University Press, 2003.

Prager, Emily. *Roger Fishbite*. Chatto & Windus, 1999.

Sagan, Françoise. *Bonjour Tristesse*. John Murray, 1954.

Schiff, Stacy. *Véra (Mrs. Vladimir Nabokov)*. Random House, 1999.

Schiff, Steven. *Lolita: The Book of the Film*. Applause Books, 1998.

Sebold, Alice. *The Lovely Bones*. Little, Brown, 2002.

Sinclair, Marianne. *Hollywood Lolita: The Nymphet Syndrome in the Movies*. Plexus, 1988.

West, Nathanael. *The Day of the Locust*. Random House, 1939.

Wilson, Edmund. *The Memoirs of Hecate County*. Doubleday, 1946.

INDEX